CLOUDIPEDIA.COM

Cloud Computing Made Easy

Copyright © 2010 by Virtual Global, Inc.

All rights reserved. No portion of this publication may be reproduced, stored in a retrieval system or transmitted in any form by any means-except for brief quotations in printed reviews-without the prior written permission of the publisher.

ISBN 978-0-557-37495-3

http://www.virtualglobal.com

http://www.teamhost.com

Table of Contents

I. INTRODUCTION 6

II. WHAT IS CLOUD COMPUTING? 10

What is "as a service"? 12

III. WHY CLOUD COMPUTING? 15

Cloud computing for end-users 15

Cloud computing for system administrators 16

Cloud computing for software developers 17

Cloud computing for IT buyers, corporate and federal 17

IV. CLOUD COMPUTING UP CLOSE 20

   A.   Cloud Infrastructure (Infrastructure-as-a-Service, or IaaS) 21
       So where is all this infrastructure? 23
       Virtualization 24

   B.   Cloud Platforms (Platform-as-a-Service, or PaaS) 26
       Cloud Platforms as Middleware 30

   C.   Cloud Software (Software-as-a-Service, or SaaS) 34

V. OTHER CLOUD OFFERINGS 36

What are "Web services"? 36

Supercomputing-as-a-Service 36

High Performance Computing as-a-service (HPCaaS) 37

VI. CLOUD AS-A-NECESSITY 40

The evolution of cloud computing 43

Why cloud computing is already becoming mainstream 44

What does cloud computing mean to me? 46

SOHO and small business 47

VII. MISCONCEPTIONS 49

Top Ten Misconceptions about Cloud Computing 49
1. The cloud is just a return to centralized computing. 49
2. The cloud is not secure. 50
3. The cloud isn't ready for enterprise users. 51
4. You lose control with the cloud. 55
5. It's the same thing as utility computing or grid computing. ... 55
6. It's only for low-end consumer applications. 56
7. It's too isolated from my other data and applications. 57
8. We won't need PCs any more with cloud computing. 58
9. Reliability will be a problem. 59
10. The cloud will give you performance problems. 59

VIII. THE "PEOPLE CLOUD" 60

Job 1.0 61

Job 2.0 62

Job 3.0 63

THE END OF THE COMPANY AS WE KNOW IT 65

The Virtual Company 66

"Jobs for Americans" 70

THE NEXT WAVE OF COLLABORATION 72

IX. GROUNDBREAKING CLOUD APPLICATIONS . 76

Healthcare applications (Health-IT) 76

Government: NASA and Nebula 80

X. THE OPEN CLOUD 83

Is open software free software? 84

XI. SECURITY AND RISKS 86

Security improvement through common security models in the cloud platform 88

Cloud computing provides superior physical security 89

THE FALLACY OF DIRECT CONTROL 91

Alternative Delivery Models 95

Accessing the cloud 96

XII. THE FUTURE OF CLOUD 99

Top ten predictions: The future of cloud computing 102

What's Next? 107

About the Authors 108

INDEX 110

I. Introduction

*PCs were a 30-year ride.
Are you ready for what's next?*

We are entering into a new era of computing, and it's all about the "cloud".

This immediately brings up several important questions, which deserve thoughtful answers: "What is cloud computing?" "Is it real, or just another buzzword?" And most important, "How does it affect me?"

In short, cloud computing is completely real and will affect almost everyone. In this day and age, we have all become stakeholders in the computing movement, and we are all affected when major changes occur. Remember how things changed when the Internet came along? Changes in computer technology seem to move at lightning speeds. It wasn't that long ago that desktop computers had 20MB hard drives and people relied on floppy disks for storage. For that matter, it wasn't that long ago that there were no desktop computers, and computing involved cardboard punch cards fed into a hopper.

It should be no surprise that another evolution is upon us once again, as there have been several since the dawn of the information age. In this book, we choose the term "era" because cloud computing is more than an evolution. Rather, we're entering the type of radical shakeup that only comes around once every 20 to 30 years: a disruptive shift in the underlying computing platform-of-choice. Remember when we moved from host computers to PCs? Now, cloud computing is shifting that computing power back to hosts again. Only this time things are different, because those hosts have become abstract, and are scattered all over the Internet... all over the world. That is to say that computing power is being shifted to the "cloud". Such a shift to cloud computing would not have been possible until now, because the enabling technology did not yet exist. Broadband connectivity now makes cloud computing a realistic possibility for not just larger companies, but for small businesses, SOHO operations, and individual consumers. These users now have the fat pipes they need to access the cloud, and they also have access now to applications and services that they couldn't begin to access or afford just a few years ago. The possibilities are growing even faster as the US government undertakes its rural broadband initiatives, which in turn will push the potential of the cloud further to the masses.

Why put applications and data in the cloud? Lots of reasons, depending on who you are: If you're just writing a document or working from home, then you can probably find online apps to do the trick without buying expensive office software. If you're an IT guy, even better—the cloud makes computing easier to manage, drives down costs (as compared to PCs and dedicated servers), and allows end-users to gain access to a broader range of applications and services. Sure, PCs and dedicated servers have served us well, but not without problems: They crash; they require us to buy, manually install, upgrade and uninstall expensive software; they become bloated, slow and loaded with viruses. Wouldn't it be so much better if someone else could take care of all the hassles? With cloud computing, we "rent" only what we need and somebody else manages the dirty work. Ask any IT person about their work schedule, and you'll find out quickly that expectations and workload often exceed the reasonable amount of time anybody really wants to work. And more importantly, ask the CFO who signs the paychecks. Do they want to cut costs? Absolutely. And cloud computing will do it—cutting costs while giving the IT staff a break at the same time.

An even greater impact in the emergence of cloud computing may be that it inspires a new wave of entrepreneurship. Nowadays, thanks to the cloud, nearly anyone can launch a genuine global business for mere pocket change. Venture funding has given way to back-pocket funding, and startup entrepreneurs no longer need $100,000 to hire a system administrator, or to buy new business software and servers. Today's emerging entrepreneurs can do everything over the Internet, and without the burden of huge up-front capital expenditures. With cloud computing, they can do more than collaborate. They can participate.

This isn't to say that cloud computing is perfect. It's not. In fact, it's not even close. It's new, and there are thousands of kinks to still be worked out. According to the National Institute of Standards and Technology (NIST) Computer Security Division, the cloud model still suffers from significant security challenges. For example, Software as a Service (SaaS) vendors are implementing disparate security approaches, raising critical questions about where data is hosted, international privacy laws, exposure of data to foreign entities, nonstandard authentication and leaks in multi-tenant architectures. These security concerns are putting mission critical data at risk, while slowing the adoption of cloud computing technologies. That's why

NIST is such an important contributor to the future of cloud computing.

> *"Everything we think of as a computer today is really just a device that connects to the big computer that we are all collectively building"*
>
> *- Tim O'Reilly, CEO, O'Reilly Media*

Whatever the case, cloud computing is here to stay. There is a popular quote attributed to Thomas Watson, founder of IBM: *"I think there is a world market for maybe five computers."* That quote assumed that computers were only for the very largest customers. We've come a long way since that speculation, and the general trend has been to move computing into the hands of everybody from big business users, all the way down to preschool children. Cloud computing continues that trend by bringing greater levels of access to high-end applications and data storage, as well as new techniques for collaboration, to even the smallest mom 'n pop businesses, telecommuters, and independent work-at-home contractors.

Mr. Watson got many things right and to his credit once again, what if his quote was saner than it once sounded? The term "cloud" refers to the computing power that is available across the Internet. In a sense, the cloud is rapidly transforming a worldwide network of computers into the largest single, "virtual" computer in the world.

II. What is cloud computing?

If the term "cloud computing" sounds confusing, then you're not alone. Cloud computing sounds like a very fuzzy term, and like a literal cloud in the sky, you can't really put your finger on it. It may help to understand WHY cloud computing is so hard to understand:

- **First, cloud computing is an extremely broad term.** It's as broad as saying "desktop computing" (i.e. the PC), which encompasses everything from the microchip to the Windows operating system to the software. As we will learn in this eBook, cloud computing encompasses all the same elements as the desktop.
- **Second, you can't touch the cloud.** Desktop computing is easy to understand because you can see, touch and feel your PC. The cloud is real, but it is abstracted to the point where you cannot see it, so it's harder to imagine.
- **And third, the term is tainted by the "me too" marketing buzz.** The term "cloud computing", for a variety of very good reasons, has become very popular, and there are plenty of new and established IT companies that want to jump on the bandwagon, often incorrectly labeling anything to do with remote computing as the "cloud".

This book is entitled "Cloud Computing Made Easy", so let's start with a simple working definition:

"Cloud computing refers to computing on the Internet, as opposed to computing on a desktop."

Hmmm, so cloud computing just means Web-based software, right? Well, no. Truth be told, a lot of major software vendors are saying "We do cloud computing too!" simply because their software works over the Internet. Far be it from the authors of this book to disagree with some of the biggest technology companies in the world, however we will disagree nonetheless. Web-enabled software is wonderful and very useful - but it has also been around for a long time. It's nothing new in itself.

In reality, cloud computing encompasses other forms of computing beyond software, including the underlying hardware (infrastructure) and platforms. In many ways, cloud computing is strikingly similar to desktop computing in that it encompasses the same three basic elements: hardware (infrastructure), operating systems (platforms), and software. The main difference is that, with cloud computing, all three elements are "rented" over the Internet, rather than being managed locally.

Let's take a closer look at the definition above:

"...computing on the Internet, as opposed to computing on a desktop."

What does it mean to say "computing on the Internet"? We simply mean that you can log onto a website to do whatever you might normally do on a PC or local server. For example, you can "rent" and manage all your hardware over the Internet, configure computing environments and/or run software. Cloud computing lets us do all of our computing on the Internet as a viable alternative to buying, installing, upgrading, uploading, downloading, backing up and otherwise managing physical hardware, operating systems and software. It doesn't require a big upfront investment, because you "rent" only what you need, and as much as you need. With cloud computing, your PC is mainly used as a way to run a Web browser. The actual processing and computing is done by remote servers (or virtual servers) and software that may be scattered across the Internet, thus the word "cloud."

In cloud terminology, the term "as a service" loosely refers to the ability to use something over the Internet on as-needed basis. The terms *software*, *operating systems* and *hardware* are confusingly described as Cloud Software (or Software-as-a-Service), Cloud Platforms (or Platform-as-a-Service) and Cloud Infrastructure (Infrastructure-as-a-Service). To make matters worse, the acronyms SaaS, PaaS and IaaS are often used. Since this is *Cloud Computing Made Easy*, we've adopted the lesser confusing terms: Cloud Software, Cloud Platforms and Cloud Infrastructure, though we will occasionally reference the other terms.

What is "as a service"?

In cloud terminology, the phrase "as-a-service" is extensively used, which simply means that a given cloud product (whether infrastructure, platforms or software) is offered in a way that it can be "rented" by consumers over the Internet. By "rented," we are implying that you pay only for whatever you use. It is often described as an "on demand" service because it is available whenever you need it. There are two immediate advantages to the as-a-service model; first, up-front costs tend to be substantially less; and second, it affords a greater level of easy scalability. For example, if you store large amounts of data on premises, you'll probably buy extra servers and storage (over-provision) to make sure that a shortage does not occur; and then when you do reach capacity, you must spend time purchasing and installing more. If you use storage-as-a-service, on the other hand, the need for over-provisioning is eliminated, and you simply purchase as much as you need on an ongoing basis, and the actual provisioning of it is transparent.

There are several methods of offering a cloud product as-a-service:

The most familiar model used by cloud software is a per user/month subscription. For example, a software provider may offer its collaboration product over the Internet for $30 per month for each user. Another approach is the advertising supported model, in which the offering is free, but you need to stare at advertisements. In such cases, the vendor receives revenues from the advertiser, rather than from the end-users. Facebook is a popular example of the seemingly free, but ad supported model.

Likewise, cloud platforms employ both the per user/month and ad supported models, as well as more creative models, such as assessing a fee per record.

Cloud infrastructure is a bit different, in that it employs the most creative as-a-service models of all, such as offering CPU time on a per hour basis, assessing for storage usage, as well as assessing for data transfers per gigabyte, often with differing rates for uploads versus downloads. Amazon's Elastic Computing Cloud (EC2) is a great example. Amazon EC2 offers a console for creating virtual machines on a per hour basis, with additional fees assessed for data transfers and storage.

NIST takes it a step further by asserting that true cloud offerings provide certain expected characteristics, which may not have been present in earlier Web-based software. These include such things as on-demand self-service, resource pooling and rapid elasticity. Naturally, on-demand simply implies that the service is available to turn on or off as needed. Resource pooling means that multiple users share a bank of servers (including storage devices and other computing resources) over the Internet, as an alternative to using dedicated servers. And lastly, rapid elasticity means the cloud offering can be dramatically scaled up and down as needed. As an example, let's pretend that a guy launches his own dotcom, and next week he is scheduled to appear on the Oprah show. Should he buy ten new servers just in case? No! If he takes advantage of cloud infrastructure, he can offer his software as-a-service, and scale it up and down as needed. With as-a-service, you only pay for what you use, and you can use as much as you want.

III. Why Cloud Computing?

To the casual end user who is just trying to get some work done there may seem to be little difference between cloud computing, desktop computing, and any other type of computing model that has been floated around over the past few decades. He or she may even use the same types of software applications to do the exact same types of things. That's the point! Cloud computing offers a better way to do the same types of things.

So then, why is cloud computing any better than ordinary desktop computing?

The answer depends on who you are.

Cloud computing for end-users

As an end user, cloud computing lets you run software applications and access data from any place and time, and from any computer; without the need to ever install, upgrade, troubleshoot software applications physically on a local desktop or server. This is one of the most important elements of cloud computing, and why it has become so popular today. In a sense, cloud computing outsources the technical hassles to someone else.

Cloud computing also makes it easier to do work anytime and from anywhere, often referred to as "ubiquitous." The old model of working involved going to the office from 8:00 to 5:00, and getting on a plane and taking a business trip or two every year. If we did work from a location outside of the office, then when we returned to the office, time had to be spent synchronizing the ad hoc work done at home with the in-office systems. Today's model of working is different. We can get just as much done at home or on the road as we can in the office. We can connect instantly to the office from anywhere in the world, gain secure access to our applications and data, and in short, *get things done* in a way that was never before possible.

Cloud computing for system administrators

Keep in mind that almost all PC owners have become system administrators in a way, unless we're fortunate enough to have access to a teenager to install and manage things for us. If your PC has ever crashed and wasted your day, then you'll understand the benefits of somebody else doing the dirty work. The problems can get out of control inside big companies, which manage thousands of software configurations, and pay employees whether their PCs work or not. The superiority of the cloud model comes in when we start to realize that desktop applications are more or less static, and cloud applications can be continuously refined. Desktop applications must be physically installed on a PC, upgraded periodically, have patches applied when they become available, and re-installed when the user moves to a new desktop or when the old one crashes. The cloud model eliminates those inconveniences. Need a new PC? Just buy one. You can still access your cloud applications without having to re-install anything. System administrators, who may need to manage hundreds, or even thousands of desktops, remote devices, servers, storage arrays and other equipment, quickly get bogged down—and the cloud model makes their lives easier.

Cloud computing for software developers

There is an even bigger advantage on the development end. Because the applications are delivered from a common code base from a central location, upgrades to the application, patches and fixes can be pushed out to the user transparently. Desktop applications require the user to actively install a patch, or at least, allow for an auto-connection to take place. Microsoft Windows uses the auto-update feature, which has become very useful and convenient, for example. However, it still requires patience on the part of the end user, who must wait for the upgrade to come in over the Internet, and then must re-boot the system for it to take effect. A cloud application, since it does not exist on the desktop, does not have that requirement. All upgrades take place on the back end, requiring no intervention, action, attention or patience from the end-user. This makes it much easier for developers to continuously upgrade their applications, and to push those upgrades out to users on a real-time basis. Going a level deeper to the platform stage, cloud computing gives developers another critical advantage. Since the platform provides developers with a common set of cloud services that have already proven to be robust, all applications are that much more stable—and quicker to completion, as well.

Cloud computing for IT buyers, corporate and federal

The critical advantages listed above have not been lost to corporate users. The ability to lessen the workload on system administrators and developers alike lets companies save dollars spent on manpower. In short, your company can do more with less, and with greater efficiency. Besides the manpower advantage, companies will also gain an advantage in terms of reduced capital expenditures. Why? The cloud not only reduces time spent on admin duties and development, it also addresses the physical infrastructure itself. Companies taking full advantage of cloud computing will enjoy a reduced need for servers and storage arrays—providing another source of savings (and in turn, reducing the system admin overhead even further).

In the corporate world, one of the most important parts of business is improving the bottom line. That's done either through increasing revenue, or by decreasing costs. When decreasing costs, the ideal scenario is to do so while still maintaining the same or better level of efficiency the company enjoyed before the decrease in costs; cloud computing provides the answer to that need. Let's take a look at a few of the dollars-and-cents statistics:

Enterprise software represents an enormous expense, as some $800 billion a year is spent on purchasing and maintaining software. The bulk of that—or about 80 percent of the $800 billion—is spent not on the actual purchase of software, but on installing and maintaining it.[1] The federal government alone spends $70 billion a year on IT systems, much of which goes toward enterprise systems. Most servers operate at only about 15 percent capacity at most times, and over-provisioning is regrettably common. Virtualization, an important element of cloud computing, allows the data center operator to make full use of server capacity. Enterprise cloud platforms can save even more.

---

[1] Peter Mell and Tim Grance. "Effectively and securely using the cloud computing paradigm." National Institute for Standards and Technology, 10-7-09.

The advantage to individuals, small businesses and large enterprises which buy software is obvious. The cost of software represents a major expense for businesses of all sizes. The presence of cloud computing options has allowed many small and midsize businesses to gain access to important features of high-end, enterprise-class software that would not otherwise be available. As a result, a major barrier to success has been dissolved, and the saga of million-dollar price tags for enterprise software is nearing an end. Large corporations will save money; and smaller companies will gain the advantage of being able to access more software resources, which were previously unavailable due to either high cost, or the software simply being unavailable for smaller implementations.

> *"If you move your data center to a cloud provider, it will cost a tenth of the cost."*
>
> - Brian Gammage, Gartner Fellow

IV. Cloud Computing Up Close

We've informally defined cloud computing as *"computing on the Internet, as opposed to computing on a desktop."* A more purist definition of cloud computing is one that differentiates true cloud computing from mere software on the Web. After all, Web software has been around for more than a decade and cloud computing is relatively new, so how can they possibly be the same things, right?

Rather, true cloud computing takes advantage of new enabling technologies and cloud constructs, which are making the movement possible. In essence, Web software has been around for years, but until recently it has been prohibitively costly for the masses to develop and host – often costing millions of dollars and taking years to develop and implement. Cloud computing changes all that by incorporating virtualization technology that allows the physical infrastructure to be rented for mere pennies compared to the old ways to engineer Web software. It further changes the equation by providing cloud-specific platform toolkits to accelerate development.

The National Institute of Standards and Technology (NIST) puts it this way:

"Cloud computing is a model for enabling convenient, on-demand network access to a shared pool of configurable computing resources (e.g., networks, servers, storage, applications, and services) that can be

rapidly provisioned and released with minimal management effort or service provider interaction."[2]

NIST also categorizes cloud computing into three "as a service" offerings, namely infrastructure, platforms and software, which are broken down in more detail here:

A. Cloud Infrastructure (Infrastructure-as-a-Service, or IaaS)

In the old days, if you needed a server, you might spend between five and ten thousand dollars or more upfront and then you'd pay a techie $30K a year plus benefits to manage it. Nowadays, with cloud infrastructures, you can actually buy a "virtual server" over the Internet almost as easy as signing up for an email account. The server never arrives at your doorstep. Instead it stays out on the cloud where you can log on and manage it anywhere and anytime over the Internet. For the techies amongst us, that means that you can buy and manage processing time (CPU time), storage, network capacity, and other fundamental computing resources without shelling out big bucks upfront. You only pay for what you use.

If you've never used cloud infrastructure, then the very notion of using a server over the Internet may sound crazy. You're probably asking the question, "How can I do that?" Well, actually, it's easy to rent computers over the Internet. The easiest way to learn is to actually do it. If you go to Amazon.com's EC2 website, you can launch and manage a real live server (well, actually a small virtual server) for an hour for about 20 cents. What a bargain! You will specify a

---

[2] Peter Mell and Tim Grance. The NIST Definition of Cloud Computing. Version 15, October 7, 2009.

server name, the type of operating system and other details to create your server instance. Then, you can log on using remote desktop or visit the website, just as if it were a real live server.

How it Works

We use the term "virtual server", because you're not really renting a physical box. That is, you can't actually walk into a room and touch your dedicated machine. Instead, it's all managed by "virtualization" software, such as VMware.

In the old days, one operating system would run on one physical box. For example, you would buy a Windows server that contained a copy of Windows, or a Linux server that contained a copy of Linux. It was one-to-one. Virtualization, on the other hand, lets you run multiple operating systems on the same box.

In the early days of virtualization, this was a handy trick. For example, virtualization made it easy to test new software on multiple operating systems without needing multiple physical boxes. Virtualization also made it easy to run Windows and UNIX programs on the same physical box, such as when a program was only available for one operating system.

Then, one day, somebody realized an even bigger trick. With virtualization, it's possible to sell the same physical machine multiple times. That is, a data center can run 10 copies of Linux on one box, and then sell it over the

Internet like different servers? Voila, the basic concept behind cloud infrastructure (infrastructure-as-a-service).

In reality, cloud infrastructure is not limited to a single server, but rather relies on a shared pool of servers, whereby any one user can scale up to take advantage of extra computing power when needed. It works because servers are mostly unused anyway, so there's always some extra computing power available if the pool is large enough. It works somewhat like a bank that loans the same money 10 times over. In theory, it wouldn't work if everyone demanded their money (or computing power) at the same time.

So where is all this infrastructure?

The cloud's infrastructure consists of actual, physical hardware that is complemented by a delivery mechanism. The main difference is that it exists outside of the user's immediate grasp, and its existence has been abstracted to the point where its exact location is both unknown and irrelevant to the users. When you work in the old way, you know that your application is located on the PC in front of you, and the data is held on the data server in the room across the hall. With cloud computing, you don't know whether your applications and data are in a data center in Des Moines or Delhi, and what's more, it doesn't make any difference.

This is an important point. One of the biggest objections to cloud infrastructure is that you can't put your finger on it. There is a certain satisfaction to walking into your server room, and being able to point to a rack of servers and storage arrays with a glorious mass of cables coming out of the back, and saying "that's where our data and applications are." But that satisfaction is an illusion; in reality, there is no inherent advantage in being able to reach out and touch your own hardware infrastructure. If it works, it works; it doesn't really matter where it lives. In fact, if your infrastructure is elsewhere at a hosted facility, then you are gaining a strategic advantage of having somebody else who specializes in such things manage it for you.

An ordinary computing infrastructure may consist of several physical pieces of hardware and cables that you must maintain and allocate. A cloud infrastructure consists of a pool of highly abstracted and scalable infrastructure devices existing in multiple provider data centers, connected over virtual private Internet connections; where a trusted third party is charged with maintenance and allocation.

Virtualization

Virtualization is the behind-the-scenes enabling technology that makes cloud infrastructure possible. Just as you can drive a car without understanding how the engine works, so too is virtualization. You don't need to know how virtualization works to use it, since it involves the infrastructure—which the end user no longer has to worry about with a cloud implementation. The concept of server virtualization allows many "virtual servers" to run on a single physical server as if each one were a separate device. Storage virtualization works the same way. Both types of virtualization essentially decouple the function from the underlying hardware, and virtualization has become a common enterprise technology for saving money and making better use of existing resources. It's not uncommon for a large enterprise to employ this technique in its own data center, and the technology is also in common use by cloud providers—delivering an efficient method for them to service the needs of multiple clients on a cost-effective and secure basis.

Why does virtualization make better use of resources? Because of technologies like *thin provisioning*. In storage for example, traditionally a volume was created for each application. This storage volume was always over-provisioned, to ensure that adequate storage would always be available; as a result, it was common for storage environments to be making use of only 30 percent or so of available storage. Virtualization uses thin provisioning to allocate storage virtually, instead of absolutely; freeing all of that previously trapped storage space. Server virtualization also makes better use of resources by not requiring separate, dedicated hardware servers for each application. In virtualizing servers, it allows for a single physical server to act as multiple virtual servers, each one separated absolutely by a virtual division that isolates each one. The "walling off" of the virtual servers within the single physical server addresses the obvious concern that there would be some potential for somebody else on the same physical server to access your data.

This is an important concept for cloud computing, since cloud computing is all about abstraction. For the end user again, the concept of applications and storage is abstracted to the highest degree—and in many cases the user will not even be aware of where the actual application or data is located. And it doesn't matter. Virtualization works hand in hand with cloud computing to provide the abstraction that is necessary for both. Virtualization provides a type of technology that allows applications to be moved around freely onto different devices that exist in the cloud, transparently to the end user.

B. Cloud Platforms (Platform-as-a-Service, or PaaS)

For most people, the term "cloud platform" is even fuzzier than cloud computing as a whole. Yet, when cloud platforms are properly understood and embraced, they potentially offer the greatest impact over any other aspect of cloud computing.

Cloud platforms can drive down software engineering costs tenfold, reduce time to market, improve profit margins, and lower risks. They can promote higher levels of security and system interoperability, and can allow system integrators to enter into new markets within days, instead of years. They can dramatically lower the skill requirements needed to create new software applications, so that entrepreneurs are empowered to serve their customers, and customers are empowered to serve themselves. In a nutshell, cloud platforms takes cloud computing to the masses.

Let's start with a simplistic understanding of the term "platform" for computing, and then we will expand our definition to the realm of cloud computing.

A platform generally refers to a "prefab" software architecture upon which you can build computing solutions. It provides core software functionality, which would otherwise need to be engineered from the ground up. Can you imagine building an oven every time you wanted to cook dinner? Probably not. Fortunately, the oven is already built; otherwise your meals would cost $500 each.

Likewise, the cloud needs platforms to do a lot of the grunt work, which otherwise needs to be engineered into every software application from the ground up at great expense. Cloud platforms serve as a launch pad for cloud software, providing "prefab" functionality such as a user interface, user sign up and administration, role-based security, federated search, multi-tenant data management and so on. If you're asking the question, "What the heck is multi-tenant data management?" then exactly! You're seeing the point. It's complicated stuff, and you wouldn't want to program it to every app. Unfortunately, most cloud developers are not talking full advantage of platforms.

By their very definition, cloud platforms are offered "as a service", meaning that you can use them over the Internet with no need to ever install, upgrade or host. Cloud platforms are readily distinguished from other platforms, which require installations, uploads, downloads and managed hosting. As-a-service means that cloud platforms are easy to use. More important, if you build cloud software on top of a cloud platform, then your solution is inherently cloud-enabled, taking advantage of underlying cloud infrastructure, elasticity and as-a-service models.

Cloud platforms also may include online tools and APIs that make it easier for developers to build on top of the platform. When choosing a cloud platform, it's important to make sure that the API is open, allowing for integration with 3rd-party, open source and legacy software and web services, otherwise, you could become overly locked into the platform provider for all your needs. This is referred to as an "open platform" versus "proprietary vendor lock-in."

Major Benefits of Cloud Platforms

On the surface, it's easy to think that cloud platforms are for software developers, but it's the IT buyers who are suffering the most from astronomical software engineering costs and delays.

For IT buyers, investors and developers, the advantages of cloud platforms are tremendous. Creating a cloud application from the ground up is a complex process, involving not just ordinary coding, but also adding a layer of abstraction, and incorporating a far-flung communications layer as well as security protocols. If every SaaS provider had to create each of these things from scratch, then cloud-based application development would be hindered, and limited to only the larger software companies. Cloud platforms address this problem by allowing developers to build cloud applications on top of an existing architecture that includes core functionality. In essence, developers can use platforms to get their software to "80-yard line" without programming, and avoid reinventing the wheel.

The benefits are many:

- **Lower costs** – In some cases, a cloud platform can reduce costs by 80% or more, because non-core code is already engineered;
- **Lower risks** – Likewise, a cloud platform can reduce risks by as much, because common functions are already tested, sometimes over a period of years;
- **Faster time-to-market** – Cloud platforms dramatically reduce time-to-market, because they serve as a launch pad for software engineering efforts;
- **Higher profit margins** – Software developers and system integration firms can deliver more for substantially less, thus higher margins on fixed price contracts;
- **Rapid prototyping** – Create and deploy concept applications without writing code;

- **Higher security and interoperability** – NIST indicates that the cloud suffers from major security issues, largely because vendors are implementing disparate and unproven security models. Cloud platforms provide a common, proven security model. If cloud software uses the platform, then it is inherently secure.

As an added advantage, cloud platforms shield both software engineers and end-users from the behind-the-scenes complexities of the entire cloud. Dan Tapscott, the author of Wikinomics, talks about the growing complexity problem this way: "the Web look[s] increasingly like a traditional librarian's nightmare --- a noisy library full of chatty components that interact and communicate with one another." He is referring to the cloud as a cluttered hodgepodge of Web apps and services, each with their own logins, data sources and security/resource functions. In the absence of cloud platforms, we are recreating the wheel millions of times over. In a few years, the redundancies will drive up costs by billions within federal IT systems, health-IT systems and other enterprise IT systems that rely on cloud services. All these IT systems will struggle with disparate security models and interoperability concerns.

Unfortunately, cloud platforms remain vastly underutilized. That's why some enterprise software systems unnecessarily cost millions of dollars and take years to implement, only to eventually fail! The resistance to platforms is sometimes baffling. It's almost as if the logic is to stick with what we know, even though it doesn't work. Ironically, some software integrators are creating totally proprietary stovepipes from the ground-up, just to avoid platforms. As a result, IT buyers are paying more than twice as much for their systems, and being locked into developers. Instead, they should be taking advantage of open APIs that are available with some of the more open cloud platforms.

Cloud Platforms as Middleware

It may also help to think of a cloud platform as the middle layer of a three-layer cake, in that it rests between the hardware and the software. Sure, you can remove the middle layer, but in doing so you're also removing a lot of important "cake" that somebody needs to bake from scratch. In the case of software engineering, that's some expensive cake. That is to say that software can be built without using cloud platforms, but the costs of doing so can be detrimental; and creates a barrier to entry for all but the largest development shops. You see – platforms actually do a lot more than just provide core functionality for software. They also lower the time and risks of engineering software dramatically because the platform engineers have already worked out the devils in the details on their own dollar.

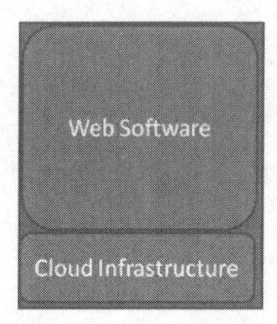

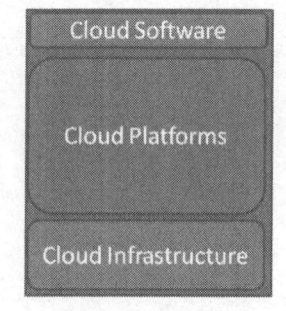

Platforms also reduce the software footprint and maintenance costs, because the responsibility for maintaining platform code is essentially outsourced to a platform provider, who achieves economies of scale by maintaining one system.

Web software that is created without platforms is considerably more costly. On the other hand, cloud platforms provide core functionality that dramatically reduces time, risk and development costs.

Types of Platforms

Cloud platforms come in many shapes and sizes, depending on the application at hand. Arguably, Google is currently dominating the consumer app platform, whereas Facebook is dominating the social networking platform, and Salesforce.com is trying to make a footprint as an enterprise software platform. Several other players, Yahoo included, offer ecommerce platforms, which have driven down the time, risk and cost of ecommerce solutions.

The term "platform" as it relates to cloud computing is often misused to refer to customizable software. Software that can be customized is simply that: customizable software. Similarly, cloud infrastructure vendors sometimes promote their products inaccurately as platforms. A platform, on the other hand, is something entirely different. A cloud platform rests between the physical infrastructure and customizable software.

Enterprise Platforms

Of all types of platforms, enterprise business platforms may provide the greatest value in the near future, simply because enterprise business systems are extremely expensive – sometimes costing $10s of millions to engineer. By enterprise business system, we're referring to the types of scalable multi-user / multi-tenant cloud-enabled software that government agencies and Fortune 500 companies spend millions on, sometimes without blinking an eye. For enterprise business systems, platforms offer such great benefit only because the engineering costs are otherwise so high, sometimes representing more than 95% of the total cost of ownership.

Significance of Platforms

In the future, cloud platforms will make the cloud easier to use. To fully understand the significance of cloud platforms, we need simply look at the evolution of earlier computing models. Can you imagine a world without desktop operating systems? We, the authors of this book, don't need to imagine. We were there.

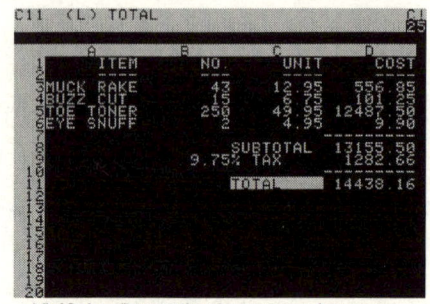

VisiCalc - Computing has come a long way.

In the early days, PCs were hard to use; and security was terrible because every software program implemented its own way of doing the same things. The early PCs were only usable by an elite community of hacker geeks or well-funded NASA engineers. They were expensive to program, because old-time developers would author hundreds of lines of source code just to move a mouse or paint lines on a screen.

Then came operating systems like Microsoft Windows and toolkits like VisiCalc. All of a sudden, anyone could use a PC. Secretaries were creating spreadsheets for their bosses. The mouse moved automatically, as if by magic. Inasmuch as some techies might knock Microsoft, their Windows platform indisputably changed personal computing. Think about it – for about $100, you get tens of millions of lines of code, which handle thousands of things that we take for granted, and which would otherwise need to be painstakingly engineered the into every software application at the cost of millions of dollars and years of development time. These days, no one in their right mind would remotely consider writing a software application directly to a PC without using some sort of platform, yet that's exactly what Web developers are doing each and every day!

The cloud platform is evolving in many of the same ways as desktop computing. Cloud platforms are helping to bring cloud software to the masses. As the cloud increases in its complexity, the role of platforms is becoming more important.

Cloud Platforms are like Operating Systems for the Cloud

We tend to think of an operating system as a behind-the-scenes technology that manages resources, and that's true. But in fact, they do much more than that. There is a major user-facing element to an operating system. Windows, for example, makes the underlying infrastructure easier to use. It provides a common user interface, a common security model, and shields users from all of those behind-the-scenes complexities.

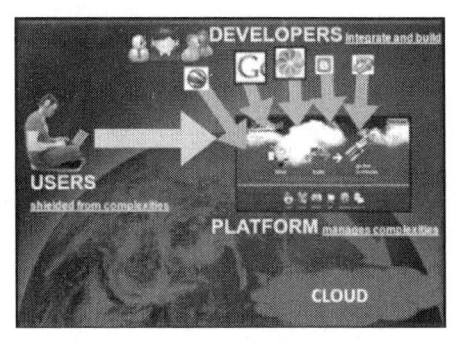

A cloud platform works the same way. The platform implements a virtual instance of a core set of functionality, with common features such as user signup, security, reporting, and so forth. The platform will then allow developers to build on top of that instance to customize it for their specific needs, and to additionally build features on top of the platform without programming, such as creation of forms, data entry collection, report writing, etc. As a result, users can log into one place and experience an integrated solution, where they do whatever they do.

C. Cloud Software (Software-as-a-Service, or SaaS)

The most important, and most visible of the three elements is Cloud Software, without which there is no need for Platforms or Infrastructure.

Again to stress, cloud computing and cloud software, i.e. software-as-a-service (SaaS), are not the same things. The two terms are often used interchangeably, but it would be incorrect to do so. Rather, cloud software is just the software part of the cloud computing triad. It is without a doubt though, the most visible part, since it faces the end user. In a purist sense, true cloud-enabled software refers only to that software which intentionally takes advantage of the of other cloud computing technologies: namely cloud infrastructure and cloud platforms.

The overall market for SaaS subscriptions, compared to on-premises software, is still young, though it is a rapidly growing niche. Because it is the most visible part of cloud computing though, it will be SaaS that drives the growth of cloud computing. Already we are seeing this growth, driven both by startups moving into SaaS offerings from the ground up, as well as established IT giants like Google and Microsoft moving into the SaaS market. Almost every major software vendor today has at least a test SaaS program in the works, and many have them in the market already.

When we talk about software-as-a-service, it usually means that the software being delivered has a common code base that is delivered to multiple users. This however, does not preclude customization. Using a common code base for SaaS applications has a big advantage, in that it allows the SaaS provider to continuously refine the program, and push those refinements out to each user on a timely basis. This not only makes for a more robust piece of software, it also allows the cost to be shared between many users. Customization however, is still allowed. Each end user may for example, be able to choose from multiple software components to create a SaaS application that very specifically meets their own precise needs; and of course, just like most types of on-premises software; SaaS applications allow each end user to apply their own user preferences and custom configuration.

V. Other cloud offerings

This section addresses other considerations of cloud computing, which didn't fit nicely into a category, and which are too important to overlook.

What are "Web services"?

The term "web services" is a bit oversimplified, and it implies that it is just a service that you access over the web. In reality, as a formal definition, web services are usually considered to be the domain of web programmers, not end users. It is a programming technique that involves use of remote subroutines, which can be called over the cloud, such s making a calculation or authenticating users. In the case of cloud computing, web services allow programmers creating cloud programs (SaaS) with ways to manage the cloud infrastructure, or integrate with other cloud programs. Using technologies such as SOAP, XML or WSDL, web services simply provide an ability to allow programmers to use other peoples' offerings over the Internet.

Supercomputing-as-a-Service

Typically thought of as the domain of wild-eyed scientists working on large-scale projects that are far beyond the scope of ordinary business, supercomputing occupies a mysterious place in the computer business. But let's draw a comparison—as recently as the 1970s, computing in general was thought to be the exclusive domain of a handful of extremely large companies and government agencies. Computers weren't for ordinary people, or even for small companies. But look where we are today. The room-sized computers of the '60s aren't even as powerful as a simple netbook. Supercomputing today is in the same place that general computing was fifty years ago.

When supercomputing meets the cloud, then its power becomes available to a much broader audience. And that's what is already happening. Maybe you can't have a supercomputer in your home—at least not yet—but you can access one over the cloud. Companies like Exa sell their supercomputing processing power over the cloud, and companies that don't necessarily have big budgets can harness the power of supercomputing environments. There are already a small number of companies that offer supercomputing as a cloud option, including the venerable Amazon, whose MapReduce offers supercomputer-like capabilities to crunch large data sets in Amazon Web Services.

High Performance Computing as-a-service (HPCaaS)

Along with supercomputing, cloud is also changing the face of high performance computing (HPC).

Supercomputing has always been expensive, often costing tens of millions of dollars. Nonetheless, they're viewed as a necessary evil by many members of the scientific community. In recent years, grid computing has gained attention as a possible alternative. The notion with grids is to take advantage of otherwise idle CPU time that's available on millions of computers. With grids, special software divvies up and "outsources" calculations to several computers in parallel, such as to PCs that act somewhat as mini-servers. Historically, grids were manually orchestrated and relied on other people's computers, which raises questions about security and privacy.

With cloud infrastructure, we have already learned that servers can be allocated dynamically as needed (as in "thin provisioning"), rather than paying for unused computing power. Then, this begs the ten million dollar question: Why can't I just harness the power of 100 servers when I need it, run a calculation and then shut them down? That way, I wouldn't need to buy a supercomputer, right?

That's exactly what HPC as-a-service does. Special HPC cloud software, including open source software like Univa UD, makes it possible to turn computing nodes on and off as needed, while orchestrating intensive calculations on those nodes. With cloud HPC, the concept is that a supercomputer never rests idle, doesn't becomes comparatively outdated in a few years, and has no hard limits on scale. The future of cloud HPC is yet to be determined. In the meantime, it will be fun to keep an eye on how the technologies mature for adoption by the serious scientific community.

Self-healing nature of cloud computing

A true cloud computing architecture is self-healing, which promotes higher uptime and less likelihood of failure. Self-healing is really nothing new; it is based on technologies that are often used in large enterprises and data centers. It simply means that should a failure occur, technology and protocols are in place to automatically correct that failure in real time. This is the heart of disaster recovery, and is part of the cloud computing model.

For the provider of the cloud architecture, this means having redundant data centers and automatic failover. For the user of cloud services, it means having constant access and guaranteed uptime to applications and data, without having to worry about recovering from data loss or disaster recovery.

VI. Cloud as-a-Necessity

Technologies become essential when they become a part of the very fabric of society. They become essential when they become *disruptive*. There are a great many new technologies that appear every year, and many of them are technologies designed to make things simpler, cheaper, and more convenient. Yet, most of them do not fall into the category of *disruptive technology*—or a technology that results in far-reaching and important changes in the way people work, think, do business, and communicate. Cloud computing is one of those disruptive technologies.

- **Cloud computing changes the way we work.** The very nature of what a "job" is, is changing. We work from home. We work as contractors. We telecommute, work from on the road, and increasingly, pay no attention to the physical boundaries of the corporate brick and mortar walls.
- **Cloud computing changes the way we think.** Old barriers are being broken down. We're no longer afraid to think outside the box, because the box no longer exists.
- **Cloud computing changes the way we do business.** The collaborative technologies that are enabled by the cloud let us take advantage of outsourcing, focusing on our core goals while letting other experts take care of what they do best on our behalf.
- **Cloud computing changes the way we communicate.** Is it necessary to get on a plane, or

drive across town for a meeting? Increasingly, the answer is no. New types of communication allow us to work closely with partners, remote employees, and suppliers around the world as if they were right there in our office.

There are objections, to be sure. There are objections to any disruptive technology. People resisted graphical operating systems. They resisted cellular phones, the Internet, and even computers as a whole, but each of these disruptive technologies won out, and our lives are better for it.

Cloud computing is fast becoming recognized as the fastest growing technology. Gartner's "Top 10 Strategic Technology Areas for 2010" lists the ten most important technologies that must not be ignored—and cloud computing is number one on the list.[3]

Cloud computing is destined to become part of our everyday lives, because it is more than technology. It's not just software that is delivered from a remote server over the Internet. Cloud computing represents a new way of thinking and doing that has become essential to stay competitive and efficient in today's economy. Here are just a few of the drivers that highlight why cloud computing has grown in importance so quickly:

- **Explosion of data.** We are truly in the "information age" today. That means we rely on information more than we ever have in the past, but it also means that there's a lot of it.

---

[3] Stephen Shankland. "Gartner: Brace yourself for cloud computing." Cnet, October 20, 2009.

- **Renewed focus on collaboration.** So what do we do with all of that data? Information is usually more valuable if it is strategically shared, not only within the company, but also with partners, suppliers, outsourcers and other stakeholders all around the world.
- **Economic necessity.** Companies face the continual need to cut costs, especially during the worst economic recession since the '30s. But even apart from the recession, global competition and other factors have led companies to embark on major cost-cutting initiatives. This involves both implementing new methods, and cutting staff.
- **Entrepreneurial activity.** The economic recession has a positive impact on entrepreneurial activity. The result is that there are more small companies today than ever before, and those small companies need access to resources at low cost. Cloud computing allows those small entrepreneurial ventures to gain access to the services they need and flourish.
- **Outsourcing.** Outsourcing and cloud computing go hand-in-hand. The outsourcing trend is driven by economic necessity described above, and it flourishes because of the intense amount of entrepreneurial activity that we're seeing, from two perspectives. Many of the small entrepreneurs that are launching their companies today are outsourcing providers. And the demand on the part of larger existing companies for cost-cutting further drives the need for outsourcing. Cloud computing provides the framework for outsourcing to exist.

- **Teleworking and telecommuting.** Yes, people are working at home, and companies are allowing it, in part out of the effort to keep costs in check. Cloud computing has provided the framework to allow a new era of working at home to become reality.

With so many factors coming into play at once, we're seeing a "perfect storm" that can have only one end result: Cloud computing becomes pervasive. In every one of the above drivers, cloud computing is what makes it happen.

The evolution of cloud computing

If you'd like to see where cloud computing is going, you simply look at the evolution of earlier computing platforms. In the 1996 documentary "Triumph of the Nerds", Steve Jobs described his early vision to take the desktop to the masses: "It was very clear to me that while there were a bunch of hardware hobbyists that could assemble their own computers, or at least take our board and add the transformers for the power supply and the case the keyboard and go get, you know, et cetera, go get the rest of the stuff. For every one of those, there were a thousand people that couldn't do that, but wanted to mess around with programming - software hobbyists."

Interestingly, today's cloud infrastructure is similar to the desktops of the '80s in several respects. Although it ultimately benefits the ordinary end user, it's mostly the techies that get excited about it and that continue to refine it. The result will be the same. Just as PCs were once seen as something "with potential" but nonetheless only used by a handful of "hobbyists" as Jobs puts it—or "geeks", to not put so fine a point on it; cloud computing is seeing the same evolution. In the future, cloud toolkits and platforms will make the cloud as easy to use as today's desktop computer; and will become as ordinary and accepted as the desktop or laptop PC.

> *"We are at the beginning of the age of planetary computing. Billions of people will be wirelessly interconnected, and the only way to achieve that kind of massive scale usage is by massive scale, **brutally efficient** cloud-based infrastructure."*
>
> --Dan Farber, Editor-in-Chief, CNET News

So where did the concept of "cloud computing" come from? It goes all the way back to the origins of the Internet itself. The Internet was always seen in diagrams as a cloud, even before the term "cloud computing" came into use. The idea was that, as described by Google's Kevin Marks, it "comes from the early days of the Internet where we drew the network as a cloud . . . we didn't care where the messages went . . . the cloud hid it from us."[4] The internet therefore gave us the first cloud, which centered around networking. Later, data abstraction added another layer to it. Today, the cloud abstracts the entire environment: infrastructure, platforms, and data and applications.

Why cloud computing is already becoming mainstream

Why do people use cloud computing? The Pew Internet & American Life Project[5] noted several reasons: 51 percent of users who take advantage of cloud computing do so because it is easy and convenient; 41 percent do so because of the advantage of being able to access data from any

---

[4] Dan Farber. "Defining the cloud." Video interview, Cnet.com. May 7, 2008.
[5] Pew/Internet & American Life Project, Op. cit.

location and any computer; and 39 percent do so because it promotes easy sharing of information. The advantages below all point to mainstreaming of the technology.

- Collaboration
- Scalability
- Better performance
- Reliability
- Simplicity

The last point, simplicity, is perhaps one of the greatest driving forces of the cloud. Let's face it, there is an element of laziness involved, and that's okay. Workers everywhere want their jobs to be easier. Cloud computing provides that. Working at home in the past, may have required a user (or the user's admin) to pre-load software into the user's home computer, and install special logins for accessing the corporate server. More often than not, that burden just led people to inaction, which resulted in fewer telecommuting opportunities. Cloud computing simplifies the entire process by removing the need for client software and by abstracting the data and application servers. Simply put, if it's easy, workers will go for it. And in the end, that helps the corporation get things done.

Business users, consumers, and software developers ignore cloud computing at their own peril. Remember when Windows first came out, and there was still a large contingent of people who insisted on sticking with the command-line interface? Those who resist the cloud model are in the same category today. Cloud computing and SaaS is increasingly impossible to ignore.

Why? Everything in computing has led to this moment. Web 2.0 technology first gave us a little taste of what true interactivity and collaboration over the Internet could do for us. While earlier Internet sites gave us information on static web sites, Web 2.0 raised the bar with blogs, social networking, instant connectivity, and a new level of interactivity over the web. Instead of just reading a web site, we could interact with it. We could send feedback. Take polls. Search for products we like, compare prices, and see what other people thought. We could hold web conferences and use things like shared whiteboards. These Web 2.0 innovations put us all in the mindset of free collaboration, unfettered by physical boundaries. Web 2.0 made it possible for the first time to hold a productive conference for example, between people in Chicago, Delhi, and London. We have gotten accustomed to Web 2.0 innovations and cannot go back to the way it was, and we want more. Cloud computing was the next logical step.

Cloud computing has gone mainstream also because of the presence of a robust infrastructure. Virtualization technology has come to the fore, and this too serves a major role in letting vendors deliver SaaS services and in letting companies gain access to infrastructure services without large capital expenditures.

What does cloud computing mean to me?

Cloud computing doesn't work unless every stakeholder has something in it for them. Every party involved can benefit, if it is implemented correctly, from the end user, to the entrepreneur, the CEO who wants to cut costs, the project manager, IT people, and third party providers.

If you think that cloud computing doesn't affect you, think again. A recent study by the Pew/Internet and American life

Project reported that 69 percent of all Internet users[6] make use of some sort of cloud computing service, and that number is growing. Do you use one of the free public email platforms like Hotmail or Gmail? Take advantage of one of the many online file storage services? Store your vacation photos online? Then you use cloud computing. The applications go far beyond those three simple examples, but the trend is noteworthy. Most people use cloud computing, even if they have never heard of the term.

These simple consumer applications of cloud computing also highlight an interesting trend. The most successful technologies are those that have penetrated both the consumer and the business markets. Cell phones, once tools of the rich and famous, are now used by everybody and can be had at any department store for fifteen dollars for a basic model. Social networking tools started out as consumer-based applications used for fun and friendship, but are now widely used as vital tools for business marketing and project collaboration. And now, cloud computing also carries equal weight in the consumer and business realms. If cloud computing hasn't touched you yet, chances are, it will in the near future.

SOHO and small business

There has been an interesting trend in software applications, which may well be coming to an end. That trend is to deliver larger and more feature-rich productivity applications, with every feature that can be imagined. In the

---

[6] Pew/Internet & American Life Project. "'Cloud Computing' takes hold as 69% of all internet users have either stored data online or used a web-based software application." September, 2008.

early days of software, this was a good approach, but today, it's rapidly reaching the status of bloatware. After a point, software in general reaches a point where it contains everything users need to function, and anything else is just fluff. But yet, traditional software vendors thrive on that fluff to give them a marketing advantage.

But is it necessary? Not always. Word processing and spreadsheet programs for example, contain far more features than most ordinary users take advantage of. We may even apply the 80/20 rule here as a casual observation: 80 percent of users only take advantage of 20 percent of the features.

The existing office applications delivered on a SaaS basis by Google, Microsoft and others are less feature-rich than shrink-wrapped offerings, but they contain enough features to be perfectly serviceable by most users. And the advantages of easy maintenance and low cost will drive more users to adopt it.

VII. Misconceptions

Now that we've decided what it is, let's look at how cloud computing has become misunderstood. Now that we've decided what it is, let's look at how cloud computing has become misunderstood. The very word "cloud" gives way to a lot of fuzzy definitions. In reality, cloud computing is just as solid and reliable as any other type of computing, the technology just refers to a mechanism to connect infrastructure, applications, and platforms over a remote network, typically on virtualized off-site servers, over a secure IP connection.

With that in mind, let's take a look at what the cloud is . . . and what it isn't.

Top Ten Misconceptions about Cloud Computing

1. The cloud is just a return to centralized computing.

The old days of dumb terminals connected to a centralized mainframe limited our computing power to one provider. With cloud computing, we can access the computing power of millions of providers from anywhere at any time, and for a fraction of the cost of host computing.

In the pre-desktop days, computing, applications, and data storage was centralized. People used dumb terminals attached to mainframes. The terminals themselves didn't hold the applications or data. Cloud computing does have that in common with the old mainframe model, in that the individual endpoints, in this case PCs or laptops, also do not hold applications or data. But there are some crucial differences. The dumb terminal used in centralized mainframe computing had no processing power; the PC does. Centralized mainframe computing connects to a central computer and storage device; cloud computing may connect to several computers and storage devices in a "virtualized" fashion.

In addition, the level of access is much broader. The centralized model required you to log in from one of the dumb terminals on the network. Today, users enjoy the unique ability to log onto their applications from any location, anywhere in the world, from a wide variety of devices, including desktops, laptops, or even smartphones; to access applications "in the cloud" and data that may reside in a remote data center.

2. The cloud is not secure.

Truth-be-told, in-house systems are often less secure, because they use unproven home-grown security models. Cloud applications developed with cloud platforms use a common security model, which lends additional security from the ground up; and cloud providers will often pay more attention to issues such as physical security and access controls.

In fact, the cloud does have several security advantages. According to NIST, these cloud computing security advantages include:
- Shifting public data to a external cloud reduces the exposure of the internal sensitive data
- Cloud homogeneity makes security auditing/testing simpler

- Clouds enable automated security management
- Redundancy / Disaster Recovery

All four points are well taken. Cloud providers naturally tend to include rigorous cloud computing security as part of their business models, often more than an individual user would do. In this respect, it's not just a matter of cloud computing providers deploying *better* security, the point is, rather, that they deploy the precautions that individual companies should, but often don't.

3. The cloud isn't ready for enterprise users.

Enterprise software need not cost millions of dollars, or take years to implement. CIOs are increasingly demanding more affordable alternatives. Some of today's popular cloud systems host tens of millions of users. The biggest concerns of enterprises rolling out mission-critical apps are flexibility, scalability and availability. The cloud has resolved those concerns.

The very term "enterprise software" is yet another one of those fuzzy techie terms that is usually glossed over. Therefore, let's break tradition and start with a working explanation: As the name implies, an enterprise software system is one that is engineered in such as way as to accommodate a very large, nationally dispersed and/or global business or organization (an enterprise). As such, enterprise software must be able to efficiently scale to handle tens of thousands, or even millions of users, and very large data sets that often exceed several terabytes.

We seem to have accepted as a painful truth that enterprise software systems are supposed to cost millions of dollars and require years to implement. Without seemingly batting an eye, Fortune 500 companies and federal agencies alike are laying out tens of millions of dollars for enterprise software systems. The federal government alone spends $70 billion a year on IT systems, many of which includes enterprise solutions. If you'd like to see examples, simply visit fedbizopps.gov any day of the week and look at some the awards that are being made to IT companies.

For good reason, many people still believe that enterprise software should cost a lot of money and time: After all, as compared to small business software applications (think of QuickBooks), enterprise software systems are much more complex, with sophisticated architectures that make it possible to accommodate such large numbers of users and scalable data sets. Buyer beware that a lot of software vendors will promote their solutions as "enterprise-enabled" simply because they use a scalable SQL backend database engine, however this is a misuse of the word. A true enterprise software system is engineered in every respect to accommodate massive scalability, by accounting for multi-tenancy, front-end scalability, dynamic provisioning and backend SQL databases with load balancing thoughtful indexing. This is not an eBook about enterprise engineering, so we won't go into any detail, except to explain by examples of the problem being solved. Example #1: What if Facebook bogged down and was too slow after the first 1000 users had signed up? Example #2: What if you needed to select from a pick-list of a million users every time you wanted to send an email to someone? Example #3: What if the human resource team could look at the finance team's data? Needless to say, all of these things would be problems, and all of these problems need to be solved.

However, the shocking truth is this: Enterprise software need NOT cost millions of dollars! In many cases, buyers are unnecessarily investing millions into enterprise software systems that could have easily been implemented for less than a tenth the time, risk and cost as compared to a few years ago. How can this be, right? Well, cloud platforms are driving down the costs of engineering by offering robust enterprise architectures as-a-service. At the same time, cloud infrastructure is driving down the costs of scalable storage and computing power by providing those things as a service.

Together, cloud platforms and cloud infrastructure are leveling the playing field. Today, approximately 80 percent of enterprise software revenues go to IBM, Oracle or SAP. What will happen when millions of entrepreneurs are suddenly able to enter the same software markets with their credit cards? In a few years, we will soon see.

The appeal to small businesses, SOHO businesses, and individual users is obvious, and this is where the early adopters are for the most part. The most obvious successes are the office suites delivered over the Web, such as Microsoft's line of subscription-based software offerings, as well as Google's Google Apps collection. Cloud computing, and the Software-as-a-Service applications that run on top of it, give these smaller users a quick and easy way to get up and running, access high-end applications, and avoid up-front costs that are typically associated with software.

But when it comes to enterprise businesses—typically defined as companies with over 1,000 employees—those cost concerns weigh less heavily than they do for smaller, cash-strapped businesses and individual consumers. Nonetheless, cloud computing applications are starting to target the mid-size and enterprise market. Traditional enterprise vendors, whose installations often run into multiple millions of dollars, are now starting to offer SaaS versions of Enterprise Resource Planning (ERP) software and other mission-critical applications.

For these larger companies, although the cost factor isn't the only consideration, it does nonetheless weigh in. A SaaS implementation of what would otherwise be a massively expensive project allows these large companies to move more gradually into ERP software, without having to implement a full-fledged "forklift" installation all at once. The risks of failure are therefore much lower. Oracle, SAP, BEA, and other well-established enterprise software vendors are all experimenting with this type of implementation.

Large-scale enterprise applications tend to be all-encompassing. Enterprise Resource Planning (ERP) systems attempt to be everything to everybody within the company, and if it's done right, it succeeds. But by trying to do so much, there is a great deal of complexity that comes with it. It's usually not possible to put in an ERP system "off the shelf." It requires customization and integration, and that's where the big costs come in. And besides big costs, the extreme amount of customization also can lead to very long rollout times, errors, or even complete failure of the implementation.

In fact, although an ERP application is large and complex, the bulk of the cost is seen in the customized development that each implementation requires. Here's where cloud computing lends a major advantage to enterprise users.

As described earlier, cloud computing is made up of three components: Infrastructure, platform, and software. The infrastructure costs (physical servers, networking and connection) are minimized with a cloud project, since the enterprise company no longer has to host their own servers for their massive applications. The platform portion of the cloud makes development easier and more robust; and the software portion of the cloud means the enterprise user no longer has to pay for continued maintenance and upgrades, and still gets to enjoy robust software applications.

4. You lose control with the cloud.

The very word "cloud" implies outsourcing to an unknown vendor; however this is a misnomer rather than reality. You can use cloud technologies internally, or outsource to a well-established vendor who has been offering reliable service for years. With the cloud, you can gain more control through a web-based control panel, while letting go of day-to-day maintenance. "The fallacy of direct control" (see section XI in this book) posits that it is more efficient to retain control over those things that matter, while freeing up your time by leaving the details to a third party expert provider.

5. It's the same thing as utility computing or grid computing.

Grid computing was an early predecessor that virtually clustered computing resources to serve a single purpose. Cloud computing has matured to serve multiple clients and multiple tasks simultaneously. Utility computing, by the same token, has evolved. Today's cloud delivers all three major elements as a service: architecture, platform, and software.

Utility computing is another term that's been widely used to describe shared access, but this buzzword also serves to muddy the waters. "Utility computing" is a term that actually predates "cloud computing," and there is some debate on whether the two are actually one and the same. In general, as we have described here, "cloud computing" refers to a broader set of services (architecture, platform, and software); while "utility computing" is generally thought of as "as a service" computing, or only the last of those three elements. Utility computing is not "the cloud", but it runs on the cloud. In that light, utility computing can be defined as the same thing as Software-as-a-Service.

One common argument that explains the difference is to say that cloud computing affords a much greater level of abstraction, while utility computing allows users to retain a greater degree of control over the physical infrastructure.

In that regard, is it necessary to retain that control? Do you *need* to know where the servers are located, and be able to tweak and fine-tune the applications? For most purposes, usually not. That is the greatest advantage of cloud computing, that the end user need not worry about the infrastructure, or indeed, even be aware of where it is located.

Cloud computing may also be confused with "grid computing," but there is a fundamental difference there. Grid computing is typically thought of as a collection of resources, such as computer servers, which may be in different locations but are virtually clustered together to address a single problem or serve a single client or single purpose. Cloud computing on the other hand, while organized in more or less the same way, serves multiple clients and multiple purposes simultaneously.

6. It's only for low-end consumer applications.

Cloud computing has gained popularity in many consumer areas, but has also gained widespread acceptance in business applications, including productivity suites, online backup and storage, and collaborative environments; with applications of enterprise-class software already being delivered over the cloud.

Cloud computing is in fact used in many consumer-facing applications, such as free email (Hotmail, Gmail), Instant Messaging, and online file and photo storage. But at the same time, it has gained widespread acceptance in many business applications, ranging from productivity applications (business application suites), to online backup and storage, and collaborative environments.

Small businesses especially have been early adopters to the cloud model, since the economic advantage allows these smaller businesses to take advantage of applications and Software-as-a-Service offerings that would otherwise be too costly for an on-premises installation.

The advantage has not been lost to larger enterprise users, however, and this represents the next wave of cloud users. Having been proven in the consumer and the small business realm, the natural progression is to larger corporate users.

7. It's too isolated from my other data and applications.

Cloud computing applications are easy to integrate with the rest of the enterprise, and already there are several integration tools on the market to make it happen.

This is another misconception, based on early cloud projects that have long since evolved. In fact, since a great many networks run over an IP backbone to begin with, cloud computing is natural to integrate with the rest of the enterprise. And since cloud-based "virtual storage" is rapidly becoming the standard as well, using an application in the cloud need not isolate the application and the data from the rest of the business. Integrating and sharing the data is straightforward.

Integrating the cloud applications themselves with existing applications running within the business however, may be a bit more difficult—but this too, is being done already. Can you run a cloud-based application that has hooks into an on-premises application? Sure. While in some cases it may take some custom integration work, already, there are several tools on the market that specifically meet this need. SaaS integration tools have already proven to be quite useful and robust in this regard.

8. We won't need PCs any more with cloud computing.

Cloud computing is a broad concept with many elements, and powerful desktops are a central part of the cloud model.

"But what about my PC?" you ask. Desktops and laptops continue to evolve year after year, becoming ever more powerful, able to hold more, do more, and connect faster. You can run some pretty powerful apps on a standard desktop computer, so why do we even need to move those apps somewhere else? Nobody wants to work on a dumb terminal any more, but don't worry. Nobody's going to take away your PC and replace it with a dumb terminal.

For many users, desktop computing may be just fine for years to come. PCs continue to serve a valuable role, having become the basis of a very large industry. Many desktop computers, desktop operating systems (which we equate to a "platform" in the cloud computing paradigm), and desktop applications, are quite productive, useful, and robust. Cloud applications will become another powerful tool in your toolbox, but the difference between today's cloud computing and yesterday's old "dumb terminal" model is that the apps are running on a more powerful client, which has multiple capabilities.

9. Reliability will be a problem.

Virtualization and platform technologies are almost as old as computing itself. What's new is the ability to market the capabilities. Cloud technologies can provide superior reliability with service level guarantees.

10. The cloud will give you performance problems.

Performance is seldom a problem with cloud computing. Latency can be minimized by selecting a provider with a data center in your own region, and by reviewing the provider's upstream carriers and service level guarantees.

VIII. The "People Cloud"

Jobs 3.0 and Decentralization of the Workplace

Cloud computing is more than a technology - it's also a game-changing business process. The reason it has gained so much traction is because of what it enables for entrepreneurs. A complete discussion of cloud computing must go beyond the technology that underlies the cloud process, to include a discussion of the greater question of what drives cloud computing, and what the social and macroeconomic impact of it may be.

In this book, we choose the term "people cloud" to illustrate how our workforce is scattering in many of the same ways that computing resources have scattered across the cloud. Even more, we are managing people resources over the Internet in many of the same ways that are managing computing resources. As a result of cloud computing as an enabling technology, we are seeing an explosion in entrepreneurship and a decentralization of larger companies.

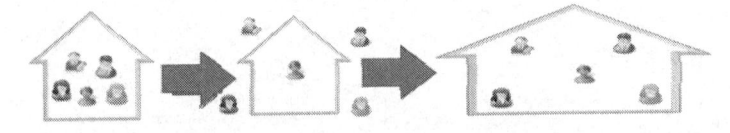

The workplace has evolved from everyone in one place, to a scattered workplace, and finally to one in which the physical roof is replaced by a virtual roof. The virtual workplace is again reconnected.

We've already seen major changes in the workplace. Companies have embraced a model of decentralization in favor of outsourcing and offshoring. Web 2.0 technologies have enabled a greater level of collaboration, which means two things: First, people no longer need to be physically present at the office, and can instead work from home, or anywhere else in the world. Second, this new level of collaboration allows companies to partner with smaller providers anywhere in the world to get the job done.

Job 1.0

The 1950's mindset of the corporation as a sort of benevolent father is obsolete. That older (and short-lived) way of doing business was what we refer to as **"Job 1.0"**. During that time, we saw the corporation as a benevolent institution, which looked out after our own well-being. We had an expectation of a 30-plus year career with a single company, an opportunity to rise from within the ranks, and a relative amount of job security. The prevailing philosophy was that company growth was equivalent to the company's apparent physical size. A company, during this time, that had 1,000 employees was considered to be more successful than one with 100 employees. Companies embraced the in-house strategy with a vengeance, and larger firms did everything from running their own internal print shops, to hosting their own cafeterias for workers.

This is in some ways reminiscent of the old-fashioned "company town," which went so far as to even provide rental housing for its workers (usually substandard), a company grocery store, and so forth, and in the process, keeping employees beholden to the company, and usually in debt to it.

Job 1.0 came with three illusions: That physical growth of a company's mass was equivalent to success, and that the "everything in-house" business model was beneficial to employees, and that it created a heightened sense of job security and loyalty.

Job 2.0

The "dotcom boom" broke down the illusions of Job 1.0. During this incredible time of entrepreneurism, the notion that a company with 1,000 employees is better and more successful than one with 100, or even one with 10, started to break down. New technologies allowed companies to do more with less. One clerk with spreadsheet software could do the work of ten people in the pre-desktop days.

What's more relevant is that Job 2.0 started to break down the illusion of a single-company career as being beneficial. The desire for a 30-plus year career with a single company became less desirable, and employees became freer to move from job to job in search of greater opportunity. The dotcom boom ushered in a new era of mobility in the workplace, and at the same time, made it more acceptable and possible for someone to go out on their own and start an entrepreneurial venture.

Still, "Job 2.0" operated under the concentrated model of corporate communities. Silicon Valley flourished, and contained an incredible concentration of talent, and more high-tech companies in one small region than anybody could imagine. That's because while the concept of "job" had evolved, the concept of "company" had not yet shifted.

Many high-tech companies during this time were short-lived, but nonetheless contributed to the collective wisdom by creating new technologies that are still used today in the latest iteration of "Job 3.0". Job 2.0 re-set the tone, breaking down the expectation of a 30-year single-company career, providing the technology for a dramatic change in how business processes are accomplished, and overcoming the '50s mindset that prevented people from switching jobs or leaving a job to go out on their own entrepreneurial venture.

Job 3.0

And so we come to the latest version of what a job really means. Today, two factors are driving a permanent shift in employment patterns:

- Modern communications technologies and cloud computing
- High unemployment and a huge recession

These new technologies mean that we now have the technological wherewithal to move away permanently from the centralized model of work and employment. Collaboration no longer requires a physical presence, and this means companies can do more with less. It means that companies are keen to outsource many of the functions that were once done in-house. This means in turn that those functions are being done by people working at home, or for small companies that specialize in specific areas.

When we speak of the macroeconomic realities and how they too have enabled the cloud computing shift, we mean that the recession has made companies take a long, hard look at how they get things done. Companies are looking for new ways to become more efficient, and they are looking for technologies that enable them to do more with less. It's not just a matter of getting new features or capabilities—it's a matter of economic survival. The economic downturn transformed cloud computing from a "nice to have" into a "must have."

The age of the cubicle is over. There are naturally some jobs that must be maintained on-premises, but increasingly, it is just as feasible to accomplish many tasks off-site, either through telecommuting or teleworking arrangements, or outsourcing to a third party provider. Today, the link between corporate size and corporate success is upside down. It is possible for a ten-person company to be more successful and productive than a 1,000 person company. And taking that to the logical conclusion, the possibility of a successful one-person company is now much more realistic than it has ever been.

The notion of working at one's own home has gone through a lot of iterations over the centuries. In the Middle Ages, it was the standard, as craftspeople and tradesmen plied their trades out of their own workshops behind their homes, but the Industrial Age brought us a new normal. Working outside the home became the standard, and people started to see working at home as less desirable. Today, the pendulum shifts once again, as new technology makes it possible to conduct business from anyplace in the world.

The idea of working from a lounge chair on the beach in a tropical island isn't that far-fetched. Or for those who don't have a tropical island handy, at least, working from home. When you call into any large company's Customer Service department for example, more often than not, you are either speaking to someone on the other side of the world, or someone who is wearing a bathrobe, sitting in their own kitchen with a laptop and broadband connection.

Ultimately, Job 3.0 has led to decentralization not only of the workplace itself, but of the workplace community. We no longer need Silicon Valley. It is no longer necessary for all those high-tech companies to be physically present in the same little section of central California. Silicon Valley has made itself obsolete. And what's more fascinating is that it has made the very idea of what a "company" is, obsolete as well.

The end of the company as we know it

Cloud computing technology and outsourcing have an obvious symbiotic relationship, and one cannot exist without the other in the real world. Outsourcing becomes much easier and more realistic when there is cloud computing; and cloud computing becomes much more than just a theoretical technology when outsourcing functions as a practical application of it.

What is a job, and what is a company? Those questions seem simple to answer, but the answer isn't always evident. Today, the answers are changing rapidly. In the last chapter, we talked about what a "job" really is and what it is becoming, now let's talk about what a "company" is. Sure, in business school they taught you all about corporate structures, and how a corporation is an entity unto itself, but that's no what we're talking about.

A "company" has always been traditionally seen as an entity engaged in commerce, which has members (owners and employees) which carry out the tasks related to the company's commercial endeavor. A larger company has "divisions" of employees, which may carry out tasks such as accounting, human resources, information technology, customer service, sales, and marketing. Seen in this way, a company is a very defined sort of organization that is self-contained. In a limited sense, every company had some interactions with other companies, as the company took on suppliers, vendors, customers, and partners, but still, it stood on its own as an island.

A company today, or "Company 2.0", operates a little differently. It is still an entity engaged in commerce, but it is no longer dependent on its internal departments and employees to carry out those tasks. Instead, a company's set of tasks is condensed down to its core mission, with all others being carried out by other companies. As such, the "corporate walls" have broken down and collaboration has built up. When a manager gets his or her weekly reports, they may not come from inside. Customer service may be taken care of by a company in Mumbai. IT is taken care of by a managed service provider in San Francisco, and marketing functions are handled by a handful of small and creative companies that collaborate with each other even further to accomplish the goals of the main company.

Web 2.0 technology, outsourcing trends, cloud computing, competitive pressure and other macroeconomic realities all have converged to make these major changes. Is a company with 1,000 employees more successful than a company with ten employees? The answer is no longer obvious. In many cases, the company with ten employees may be able to accomplish the same thing, reach the same sales goals, and carry out the same tasks as a much larger firm with many more employees.

The Virtual Company

Taking the concepts described in the previous section a step further, we can easily see the shift that has occurred from a workplace organizational structure that was several layers deep, to one that is leaner in nature, but incorporates a "cloud" of virtual extensions. In the past for example, a hierarchical business would include internal departments for data entry, payroll, public relations, IT programming, and so forth. In addition, the same business would retain functions like data storage, telecommunications, web hosting, and server farms internally as well.

The inherent inefficiencies of this hierarchical model are obvious.

The boundaries of the actual "company" have become permeable to the point of being nearly invisible. As a result, we are already seeing the emergence of the "virtual company." These companies exist in reality today all over the world. A "virtual company" has no corporate walls at all. It may be organized to formally have only one or two employees, yet it may have dozens, or hundreds of people working towards its main commercial goal. The CEO's office may be a spare room in her house; the "Marketing Department" is actually a virtual group of creatives working in spare rooms of their own, servicing not only the primary virtual company, but several others as well. The entire network of people—we can no longer call them "employees"—are connected in real time through modern collaborative technology, and the entire IT infrastructure exists in the cloud. Virtual private networks (VPNs) ensure that every party can connect to the applications and data they need on a secure basis, from any location and from any machine. At any given time, the Public Relations manager may be working out of a Starbucks, the tech support guy is sitting in his kitchen wearing a headset and nibbling on leftover pizza as he doles out advice, and the Vice President of Operations is keeping everything flowing smoothly from a bungalow on the beach in Thailand. Indeed, it is very possible that most of the members of this "virtual company" have never even met face-to-face. And they don't need to.

Why does a company outsource?

A company engages in outsourcing because it brings cost savings and efficiencies, and because it has the technological framework to do so efficiently through innovations in cloud computing.

But the bigger question is, does it really make a company more cost-effective and efficient? Since traditionally, we think of achieving gains as something that is done through control, but this is not always correct. Outsourcing actually serves the broader goal of efficiency by breaking down those artificial corporate barriers, exposing processes so that they are more transparent and responsive to the corporate entity, and eliminating unnecessary layers of corporate bureaucracy.

A highly vertical company, which tends to do all functions in-house, will out of necessity have enormous layers of bureaucracy. Processes get bogged down. Reporting may not be responsive enough. Individual fiefdoms within the corporation may have conflicting goals, and may be so caught up in their own domain that they neglect the greater goal of the corporate entity. When a company is so large and organized vertically in this way, it may very easily lose focus and lose its ability to respond to the market quickly and efficiently. As such, the economic advantage is not the only advantage—a less integrated company will simply be able to respond better, maintain its core focus better, and spend its money better.

What makes a good company to begin with? A company that specializes in something; a company that does something or produces something better than anybody else. When a company starts devoting large amounts of energy and resources to tasks that are not related to that thing it does better than everybody else, then that company's energy starts to dissipate. And more importantly, those peripheral tasks aren't getting done as well.

For example, a company that makes pizza may make the best pizza in town. They're good at it. That's their "thing." But there are other things they're not as good at. Good pizza makers aren't necessarily good marketers, and so that pizza company outsources the marketing function to another company, which is very good at what *they* do.

"I've been outsourced!"

That's become a common cry of the working person in today's world. And yes, it's real, and it happens every day. A company decides to outsource a particular function, and the internal staff are let go. Opponents of outsourcing incorrectly assume that when a job is outsourced, it is lost, and therefore contributes to the overall rise in unemployment and contributes to the overall detriment of the economy.

This is not the case. Outsourcing does not necessarily result in job *loss*. It results in job *shifts*. A programmer today for example, will gain greater job security and higher pay by working for a programming job shop, rather than an internal corporate IT department.

The proven benefits of outsourcing are undeniable, and the market reality is that it is here to stay. The appropriate response is to see it not as a challenge from a work perspective, but as an opportunity, as indeed it has proven to be so. Opportunities exist as a direct result of outsourcing—opportunities for employment at outsourcing service bureaus, and opportunities for individuals to work independently, or to start their own entrepreneurial service bureaus.

"Jobs for Americans"

Another common battle cry of opponents of outsourcing, this complaint assumes incorrectly that when a job is outsourced, it is outsourced overseas. And while many tasks do indeed go to India, Vietnam, Russia, and other third world and emerging nations, plenty of those tasks do stay at home.

Why they do stay at home is simple supply and demand. Because we are in the era of Job 3.0, there are more former employees who have moved towards being independent contractors, freelancers and consultants, telecommuters, teleworkers, and work-at-homers. The supply of domestic third-party businesses offering services to other companies that wish to outsource has increased, making it very easy indeed for companies to take advantage of outsourcing (through cloud computing technology), while still keeping jobs within the geographical boundaries they call home.

There is no question that some of the tasks go offshore, but that is one cloud that has a silver lining. Here's why.

India has built much of its economy on IT outsourcing to US and European companies. Manufacturing is now frequently sourced to companies in China, and more recently, Vietnam. When this occurs, the immediate result is the loss of an American job. Those who do not favor outsourcing because of social and political reasons fail to look beyond that immediate impact, however. Yes, there is an immediate job loss, but what is the net result?

- First, the company doing the outsourcing can cut costs, which is important to its long-term survival. The company's outsourcing strategy will help it to remain profitable, and therefore able to stay in business and keep in place the jobs that still exist. In other words, outsourcing certain processes and jobs allows for the retention of other jobs.
- The third-world or emerging nation raises its own standard and increases the ranks of its own middle class. That country then becomes a more viable trading partner for the United States and Europe. The citizens and workers of those emerging nations, having raised their own standards of living due in large part to the presence of outsourcing, gain an appetite for consumer goods—and more often than not, consumer goods that are made, sold and distributed by Western companies. Walk into any shopping mall in downtown Bangkok, Beijing, or Moscow, and you'll see aisles full of Western chains, Western brands and Western products. Raising the standard of living of emerging nations therefore creates a positive feedback, giving greater opportunities for Western companies to supply and trade with emerging nations, and creating more jobs in the process.

Strategies of isolationism have always been popular with a certain subset of the citizenry, but they have always been a failure. Is it really necessary to keep opportunities from third world countries and keep them impoverished, in order to promote our own success and wealth? Absolutely not. Free trade and outsourcing benefits everybody.

The next wave of collaboration

Cloud computing isn't just about delivering software-as-a-service. Cloud computing has given us a whole new way of collaborating.

What did collaboration mean in the 1950s? It meant walking over to the conference room and chatting about a project with your colleagues over coffee. Maybe it meant picking up the phone and calling your supplier to discuss your needs, or getting on an airplane and flying across the country for a face-to-face meeting.

But collaboration means more than talking, it means sharing information and data. In the 1950s, sharing information and data was a very physical, and labor-intensive process. Shared data may have come in the form of reams and reams of printed reports that were sent via special courier, but still, collaborating on a project required a lot of face-to-face interaction. The only way for two people in different offices to work on a design, a spreadsheet, or a document together, was to sit down in front of the same document at the same time, in the same room.

The information age has given us a lot of things, but chief among those is a whole lot more information. That translates to enormous amounts of data. Now office politics is a strange thing, and people tend to be protective of their own work areas, their own projects, and their own information. This tendency, along with a lack of collaborative technology, led to "data silos", or independent areas of data that were useful for specific purposes and in specific areas, but were inaccessible outside of a very narrow scope. The existence of data silos meant that there was a lot of redundant effort going on in a big company.

Two things have happened to break through that data silo mentality. First, the sheer explosion of data has made it impractical; and second, cloud computing and collaborative technology has made it possible to open up those silos and allow for data sharing to take place. Data that was previously held in independent silos in corporate fiefdoms throughout the enterprise must be shared and constantly revised and updated by many different people in different locations. This sharing isn't possible without some sort of collaborative technology that exists "in the cloud," which allows for instant and easy communication regardless of location, easy sharing of data, and easy collaboration on projects.

Progressive collaboration

As we have progressed from "Job 1.0" to "Job 2.0" and "Job 3.0", collaborative technology has progressed in the same way. Those ERP applications we talked about earlier represented some of the first attempts at large-scale collaboration. And while they did provide for some collaboration, data sharing, and a unified view of information, the costs were enormous.

Middleware offered another approach to collaboration, although this too had limitations that were based on each proprietary middleware platform. Integration afforded through middleware platforms is often limited to certain applications or data types.

Other types of Web 2.0 collaboration overcame the data formatting limitations of middleware, and tools like wikis portals or mashups stepped in to allow for greater access through a common Web-based interface.

Cloud computing moves collaboration a step further, and brings together the benefits of all three. Like Web 2.0 mechanisms, access can be nearly universal. Participants can collaborate from virtually anywhere, and depending on the cloud application and the interface, may not even have to have any special client-side software installed. Like middleware, cloud computing creates an environment where applications and data can be more easily integrated. And like ERP applications, it can be used to present a unified view of information.

The New Openness

The reality of corporate life, for anybody that has ever worked in an office, is that any large company tends to develop "islands" over time. Fiefdoms. Independent areas of domain into which others dare not tread. As corporate people, we tend to be protective over our own areas of work. But although this seems to be human nature, it is counter-productive to the corporate goal.

This tendency results in a lack of cooperation, and it results in redundancy of work. Early on, redundancy was often necessary simply because of technological limitations. The Operations Department, Customer Service Department, and Accounting Department all need information on customers, and all three probably had their own databases of customer information, which were completely stovepiped and inaccessible to anyone outside of that specific department. Relational database technology and simple networking made that model unnecessary, yet it still exists. Companies that have overcome this mentality operate more successfully. Simply put, it's often efficient to share data. Of course, all the usual security precautions, authentication and authorization are in place, but the data gets shared with who needs to see it.

Let's extend that to a broader view. We've seen that companies are no longer constrained by physical boundaries, and a company's mission is better carried out by an interacting subset of many different companies, individuals, teleworkers and partners. This too can present an information bottleneck. Yes, we have networks for sharing information within the corporate boundaries, but what about outside the corporate boundaries? This too, is starting to melt down. For example, some of the country's largest retailers have supplier networks that allow vendors to connect securely and directly into the retailer's inventory database. The vendor can see when a particular product is low, and trigger a replenishment order automatically. A cloud-based approach to data and applications allows for data and applications to be shared whenever appropriate, with whomever appropriate.

IX. Groundbreaking cloud applications

Cloud computing is a classic "disruptive technology" that is destined to change long-standing processes across all industries. Two of the most groundbreaking cloud-based applications that will occur over the next few years are in healthcare, specifically in electronic health records and healthcare informatics; and in government applications.

Healthcare applications (Health-IT)

The current administration continues to be aggressive in pursuing healthcare reform. Aside from the issue of universal health insurance coverage, which has gained the greatest coverage in the media, the reforms include much more under the hood. Most notably, this means implementation of electronic health records, and the creation of a nationwide health care infrastructure that would make it easier for healthcare providers to share and access patient records.

Part of this plan would create a National Health Information Network (NHIN), which is a broad, interoperable platform for sharing electronic health information. The NHIN would connect providers, insurers, and emergency responders.

According to the Department of Health and Human Services, the government's health care informatics plan's goals include:[7]

"Medical information will follow consumers so that they are at the center of their own care

Consumers will be able to choose physicians and hospitals based on clinical performance results made available to them

Clinicians will have a patient's complete medical history, computerized ordering systems, and electronic reminders

Quality incentives will measure performance and drive quality-based competition in the industry

Public health and bioterrorism surveillance will be seamlessly integrated into care

Clinical research will be accelerated and post-marketing surveillance will be expanded."

The concept of electronic medical records (EMR) and patient health records (PHR) is one that has long been discussed, and is already in use in other countries. There is no doubt that it will be part of the current administration's broad health care reform initiative, and there are already legislative incentives in place to encourage health care providers to get with the program. EMR doesn't just mean that the hospital puts your patient records in their computer—it means a new level of sharing. This of course, is within the HIPAA regulation framework and assumes a rigorous level of security, but it allows for a cloud-based infrastructure to exist for EMR. The benefits are obvious. A

---

[7] US Department of Health and Human Services.

patient's medical records would be available to any authorized health care provider, anywhere in the country. You could travel anywhere you want, and your records go with you. Any authorized provider could access your records in case of an emergency. Already, there is a common but limited version which has shown great benefit—many of the large drugstore chains keep customer records in a secure database, so that you can go to any branch, anywhere in the country, and receive your prescription. The database also includes relevant information such as drug interactions and allergies. This is only the tip of the iceberg. Ultimately, this limited drugstore application will be integrated with all other healthcare providers. What's the result? It could save lives. Error rates would be reduced, and caregivers will have more information at their disposal when making critical decisions about your care.

This technology, based strongly in cloud computing technologies, is rapidly gaining momentum. The RAND Corporation, in testimony presented to the Senate Finance Committee, highlighted just a few of the potential benefits of a cloud-based healthcare IT (HIT) system rolled out on a national scale:

"The hope of many is that the broad adoption of HIT systems with the aforementioned functionality in the United States will transform health care in terms of making it more efficient and effective simultaneously. Efficiency would be enhanced by reduced test duplication, improved drug utilization, better scheduling, reduced paper record handling, and improved claims processing and billing. Effectiveness would be enhanced by reduced errors (reduced handwriting-based errors, for example), reminders to improve preventative care, decision support for better evidence-based practice, improved management of chronic illness, and improved continuity of care for those patients seeking care away from their primary provider (such as was needed to support the mass evacuation that occurred after Hurricane Katrina). Effectiveness would also be enhanced by the quality of care assessment such systems would make possible and by improvements in the evidence base for best practices derived from the analysis of large electronic medical record databases."[8]

The potential social benefit is clear. Not only would individual hospitals benefit by moving to a more technology-based patient record system, society as a whole would benefit by integrating those systems together in a national database that relies on secure cloud computing technologies.

Besides the advantage of better patient care, cost savings would be enormous. In this day and age when the health care debate is often framed in terms of dollars and sense, a cloud-based national patient record system is an obvious element that should be included. RAND Corporation claims that savings that could be achieved would reach $80 billion per year, assuming a 90 percent adoption rate by hospitals and physicians. To put that figure in perspective, it's a full four percent of the $2 trillion spent annually on health care in the United States.

The benefits can also be seen just looking narrowly at adverse drug events. Every year, there are errors in

---

[8] RAND Corporation. "The potential benefits and costs of increased adoption of health information technology." Richard Hillestad, July, 2008. Testimony presented before the Senate Finance Committee on July 17, 2008.

medication that result from lack of allergy or drug interaction warnings, handwriting errors, and poor dosage monitoring. The RAND study further estimates that the safety benefit would be enormous, avoiding as many as 2.2 million such adverse drug events per year, saving nearly $4 billion per year.

Could these savings be achieved without a cloud computing infrastructure? Not likely. The great benefits illustrated by RAND cannot be achieved if those electronic records are stovepiped, retained only by each individual provider. The cloud-based infrastructure suggested by the DHHS brings the scope of the proposal into greater perspective, delivering the benefit on a much wider scale, and allowing for the greater level of benefits that result only from data sharing to exist.

Government: NASA and Nebula

Much as we all like to complain about government inefficiency, hulking bureaucracies and outdated procedures, there are a few areas where government really does excel in setting the standard for the rest of the country. In the area of public access to documents over the Internet for example, the Feds have done quite well. It's no longer necessary to drive downtown to a government office, or make a phone call and wait a week for a clerk to mail a form to us—we can just download it over the Internet. Even state Departments of Motor Vehicles—well known and maligned for hour-long waits and grumpy employees—have gotten onto the bandwagon of technology, and in most states it's now possible to renew your license plate online or at an automated machine in the office lobby. And once again, it may well be the government that sets the pace for embracing the cloud computing model.

It's not surprising that the biggest cloud project in government comes from NASA, an agency that always tends to be out in front of the pack with new technology. A cloud computing pilot called Nebula, being developed at the NASA Ames Research Center, "integrates a set of open-source components into a seamless, self-service platform, providing high-capacity computing, storage and network connectivity using a virtualized, scalable approach to achieve cost and energy efficiencies." NASA says that Nebula provides for rapid development of applications that are both policy-compliant and secure, promotes collaboration, and encourages reuse of code.

Nebula is a wonderful example of cloud computing done right. It is open source, which means it is transparent and highly interoperable. It is a full, true cloud system that incorporates infrastructure, platform, and software; all three of the main components of cloud computing. Nebula is already in use for educational and public outreach uses, collaboration, and mission support. Amateur astronomers use it to upload high resolution photographs, and the LCROSS participation site, where amateur astronomers work with NASA scientists to get a better view of the moon, is built on the Nebula platform.

Two useful elements of Nebula elegantly illustrate the benefits of cloud computing. It automatically increases computing power and storage as the web application needs it. This is a central benefit of cloud computing in general—the user need not worry about compute power and storage, since that's all automatically and transparently taken care of on the back end. When more storage space is needed, it's allocated. If more compute power is needed, you get it transparently. Second, Nebula addresses the security worry.

It was built to be secure, as well as compliant with government policies (of which there are many).

The Federal CIO Vivek Kundra, who was formerly the District of Columbia technology chief, has been a strong proponent of use of cloud computing in government as a way to gain efficiency and save taxpayer dollars. In Washington DC, he was able to eliminate a $4 million initiative to create an intranet for the DC government, and instead, shift the district government to Google Apps—accomplishing the same goal, and saving a huge amount of money. Kundra's move to the cloud enabled DC to save money and improve efficiency. For example, now the district's training information can be obtained through online videos on Google Apps; the same Google Apps is also used to add more transparency to government by making procurement data available to the public. Kundra claims that "The cloud will do for government what the Internet did in the '90s. It's a fundamental change to the way our government operates by moving to the cloud. Rather than owning the infrastructure, we can save millions."[9]

---

[9] Gautham Nagesh. "Local technology czar could be headed to Obama administration." Nextgov, November 26, 2008.

X. The Open Cloud

Open source software has in general been on the rise, and there's no doubt that it delivers many benefits to developers and end users alike. There are numerous cloud computing services that are either written entirely in open source code, or at least incorporating open source into the final application. Two of the biggest advantages of open source are lower cost, and greater flexibility, and these benefits fit well into the entire cloud computing paradigm, which delivers the same. Open source in short, enhances cloud computing's promise to deliver greater cost savings and flexibility to those who use it. It does this through two means: First, by streamlining the development end by allowing developers the use of existing open source code rather than "reinventing the wheel." This model correlates closely with the use of a cloud platform, which also allows cloud applications developers to build applications on top of an existing application infrastructure, so that routine functions need not be built from scratch. Doing so not only provides an advantage in terms of reduced development cost, it also has the advantage of allowing the developer to access code that has already been proven. In this respect, cloud computing applications, particularly cloud computing applications that have been built using open source components, is more likely to be robust and possess fewer flaws than an application built entirely from scratch from the ground up.

Second, the open source paradigm answers the question, "What happens to my cloud application if the provider goes out of business?" If cloud-based applications are based on open software models, then if and when a cloud provider goes out of business, an individual client could easily take over their own applications if necessary, or transfer them to another provider.

Is open software free software?

Here's a quick answer to that question: No. Casual observers often confuse these two very separate software movements. The "free software" movement is an ideological platform that suggests that all software should be free, and it is only practical in a very limited sense. The "open source" movement is a technological platform that espouses open development, because it allows for advantages such as continuous improvement of the code base, and easier customization for individual users. The latter is practical in almost all cases of software development

Here's a useful description from GNU:

" The two terms describe almost the same category of software, but they stand for views based on fundamentally different values. Open source is a development methodology; free software is a social movement. For the free software movement, free software is an ethical imperative, because only free software respects the users' freedom. By contrast, the philosophy of open source considers issues in terms of how to make software 'better'—in a practical sense only. It says that nonfree software is an inferior solution to the practical problem at hand. For the free software movement, however, nonfree software is a social problem, and the solution is to stop using it and move to free software."[10]

This is an interesting concept, and fascinating fodder for ivory tower discussions in university seminar rooms and coffee houses, but ultimately an impractical one. Ultimately, it is true that open software is indeed a methodology used to make software technologically superior, but the above argument of course eliminates incentive to make the software in the first place.

Open source delivers the advantages of:

- Flexibility to adapt and customize software to suit individual needs
- Lower cost of development
- More robust development due to continuous revision

Free software, on the other hand, constrains development by limiting that development only to academics, hobbyists and people with too much time on their hands, and would eliminate an entire class of development professionals who create software for a living.

We advocate the use of open source in cloud-based platforms as well as cloud-based applications for the above advantages, and most importantly, to overcome the potential drawback of cloud providers going out of business and leaving proprietary applications, which companies may have come to depend on, inaccessible.

---

[10] Richard Stallman. "Why open source misses the point of free software." Free Software Foundation.

XI. Security and risks

Security is incredibly important in today's environment. Cyber-attackers and other types of black hat folk want to infiltrate your network, often for personal gain, and the losses every year due to cyber-attack are enormous. We take great measures to protect our data and our networks with firewalls, anti-virus and anti-malware software, physical protections such as locked data centers, and sophisticated authentication and authorization techniques.

Any good IT security manager is paranoid, and the belief that "everybody is out to get me" is one that serves the IT security mission well. "Trust no one" is the watchword. The poor IT security manager is as a result often resented by end users, who must comply with regular password changes, policy items that may be annoying or inconvenient, and procedures that may make access more difficult. And the payoff isn't always obvious, since the most ideal outcome for the security manager is that "nothing happens."

It is only by looking at what happens to other people, and statistics related to loss and frequency of attack, that we realize that the security investment is a good one. The 2008 CSI Computer Crime and Security Survey shows that there is an average reported annual cost of nearly half a million dollars for financial fraud, $350,000 for dealing with "bot" computers in the network; and an overall average annual loss of just under $300,000. Twenty-seven percent of respondents said they had detected at least one targeted attack.[11]

It's interesting to note though, that the security issue has its own cloud-based solution that is growing in popularity. Security is increasingly delivered as a managed service by a third party provider, a factor that gives weight to the relevance of cloud computing and "as a service" offerings in respect to the security question.

There are several obvious reasons why security is being delivered, quite successfully, on an outsourced basis through the cloud. Like many other types of services that are delivered over the cloud, security is a specialized field. Many smaller companies especially lack the high-end expertise required to run security in-house, and having access to the best security experts in the business from a third-party provider will afford those companies better security, more expertise and knowledge, and access to higher-end security applications and equipment than they could provide on their own.

What happens when data and applications are put into the cloud? Do we lose control over the security precautions? What happens to security? Those are fair questions that must be addressed. The word "cloud" implies by its very nature that the exact physical location of data and applications may not even be known. The abstraction provided by the virtualization technology used by cloud providers makes physical location even harder to pin down.

---

[11] 2008 CSI Computer Crime and Security Survey.

Security improvement through common security models in the cloud platform

One unnecessary limitation to cloud computing is that at present, cloud application providers tend to implement their own proprietary security approaches. This gives rise to a number of concerns and questions concerning international privacy laws, exposure of data to foreign entities, stovepipe approaches to authentication and role-based access, and "leaks" in multi-tenant architectures. These security concerns have slowed the adoption of cloud computing technology, although it need not pose a problem.

The very nature of a cloud platform is that it imposes an instance of common software elements that can be used by developers to "bolt on" to their applications without having to write them from scratch. This advantage is especially useful in the area of security. The cloud "platform as a service" brings an elegant solution to the security problem by implementing a standard security model to manage user authentication and authorization, role-based access, secure storage, multi-tenancy, and privacy policies. Consequently, any SaaS application that runs on the common platform would immediately benefit from the platform's standardized and robust security model.

Understanding how operating systems work can provide a good point of reference. An operating system, such as Windows, OS X, or UNIX, has security features built in. The operating system vendor constantly makes refinements to their own security model, which are issued in regular updates and patches. Individual applications therefore, need not worry about addressing those security issues. Now of course, relying solely on the operating system's security features is poor practice; most users will add in firewalls, anti-virus software, encryption, or one or more methods of authentication and authorization. But, the basics are already taken care of.

Cloud platforms work the same way. When a developer builds a cloud application on top of a cloud platform, they benefit from the platform's existing common security model.

Cloud computing provides superior physical security

This may seem to be a counter-intuitive argument. Yet lack of physical security is the cause of an enormous amount of loss. In a GAO report on NASA cybersecurity, it was noted that a stolen laptop had data on it that was subject to arms traffic regulations.[12] This is by no means an isolated incident, and stolen laptops are a surprisingly common source of data loss.

And it may surprise the reader to know that loss is often the result of internal attack. Yes, insiders account for much of the losses that occur. Industrial espionage is a reality. And while the specter of black hats hacking into your network from a third world country is very much real, very often, the "black hat" is in reality a trusted employee. It's the guy from the Accounting department who you have lunch with. It's the lady who brings you coffee in the morning and always remembers that you like two sugars. It's the recent college grad with so much potential, who did such a great job on that last report.

---

[12] Michael Cooney. "NASA network security torched." NetworkWorld, October 15, 2009.

A survey by The Strategic Counsel sponsored by CA actually showed that internal threats are a bigger threat than attacks from outside.[13] The survey showed that internal security breaches are increasing, even while other threats are decreasing. Forty four percent of respondents indicated that internal breaches were a major challenge.

Of course, insiders can attack your network and data regardless of where it is located, given enough incentive and information, but physical proximity of the actual hardware and data makes it much easier to gain access.

There are several security advantages to the cloud. NIST defines these advantages as follows:

- Shifting public data to a external cloud reduces the exposure of the internal sensitive data
- Cloud homogeneity makes security auditing/testing simpler
- Clouds enable automated security management
- Redundancy / Disaster Recovery

All four points are well taken. Cloud providers naturally tend to include rigorous security as part of their business models, often more than an individual user would do. Most IT directors and CIOs understand that disaster recovery should be a part of their environment, but still, other things get in the way and disaster planning gets put aside. Or worse, a company implements a minimal disaster plan policy, which is then shelved and forgotten until it is out of date.

---

[13] "Survey: Internal security threats outpace attacks from external sources." Contingency Planning, July 17, 2008.

According to a recent British survey, 52 percent of organizations had specific business continuity plans. But, despite increasing awareness, companies remain complacent about it, and only 64 percent of managers say that business continuity is seen as important to their organizations.[14] But while many businesses neglect business continuity and disaster planning on their own, they surely expect it to be provided when a third party is handling their data, and cloud providers as a rule will incorporate disaster planning far more than will an individual company, also including specifics of it in their service level agreements.

In this respect, it's not just a matter of cloud computing providers deploying *better* security, the point is, rather, that they deploy the precautions that individual companies should, but often don't.

The fallacy of direct control

In looking at the security of cloud computing, it is necessary to look at the alternative, and the inherent risks of non-cloud computing. It's a natural human tendency to want to have control over everything. And if somebody else is controlling something, we want to look over their shoulders while they're doing it. When the plumber comes to fix our pipes, do we sit in the living room and watch television and let the poor guy just do his job? No, of course not. We follow him to the bathroom and watch.

---

[14] Chartered Management Institute and the Cabinet Office. "A decade of living dangerously: The business continuity management report of 2009." By Patrick Woodman and Dr. Vidal Kumar, March, 2009.

It doesn't make the pipes get fixed any faster or any better, but by watching, we have regained that sense of control that we lost when we called the plumber in the first place. It's almost as if by watching the plumber, we're doing the work ourselves. We are no longer in control, but we *feel* as though we are.

In the case of the busted water pipe for example, is it better to maintain direct control over the situation? Probably not. Most of us who are not plumbers have better things to do with our time. And while it's true that we could probably fix that broken pipe ourselves if we had enough time, how-to manuals, and pipe dope, the plumber (who's done it many times before) could probably do it faster and better.

We can see in this simple scenario that there are circumstances where it is better to *not* have direct control.

For those who resist using the cloud, the alternative is to remain *in control* by running your own data center, your own servers, your own storage farm, and your own applications. Doing so leaves you in complete control, but there is an opportunity cost involved.

The guy who fixes his own plumbing suffers an opportunity cost, because he must make multiple trips to the hardware store, invest time and money, purchase hundreds of dollars' worth of tools, and miss his favorite television show. And just like the guy who fixes his own plumbing, the company that insists on hosting absolutely everything in-house is losing out.

CLOUD COMPUTING MODEL	IN-HOUSE MODEL
Little or no capital investment	Large up-front capital investment
IT staff free to attend to other concerns	Requires IT staff to attend to servers, applications, etc.
Service level guarantee	Nobody to blame but yourself
Physical security included	Extra physical security required
Security built into cloud platform	Additional security tools must be deployed and maintained
Backup and disaster recovery included	Must deploy backup and disaster recovery protocols

The most immediate advantages of the cloud is the lack of an up-front capital investment, and freeing the internal IT staff to attend to more pressing concerns. But beyond that, there are advantages that relate directly to security. A cloud computing service provider will typically offer a service level guarantee to protect against data loss, outage, failure, and cyberattack. Typically, this SLA is backed up by specific terms that lay out performance levels, as well as penalties that the provider may be liable for if those levels are not met.

The physical security element is important and often overlooked. All the firewalls and passwords in the world are useless if somebody in a lab coat carrying a clipboard can bluff his way into your office and walk out with a pocketful of thumb drives and the CEO's laptop under his arms. And make no mistake, this *does* happen, and often. Industrial espionage is alive and well. If you are hosting your own data center, is your data safe? Sure, it's firewalled. But is it in a locked room? Is access to that room regulated, with entry by keycard only? Probably not. Service providers offering cloud services, collocation centers and hosting providers typically adhere to rigorous physical security protocols to protect against physical theft or tampering.

Besides physical security, the technical security is of the utmost importance. Hosting your own servers and applications requires extra measures. A larger organization may need to deploy dedicated IT staff to security only. Cloud computing, on the other hand, builds security directly into the cloud platform. While the company still must maintain in-house security in any case, the provider ensures that the applications and data are safe from attack.

And lastly, the issue of disaster recovery is vital, and one that is often ignored. We may tend to think that simple backup is equivalent to disaster recovery, but it is not. Disaster recovery calls for redundant, off-site backup, as well as procedures and technology for recovering data and applications at a moment's notice in case of disaster. It can be costly—but a cloud provider will already have these measures in place.

Of course, when considering cloud providers, these considerations are always a factor, and it should be determined ahead of time that the cloud provider:

- Offers a detailed, specific SLA
- Offers physical security at their data center
- Offers superior technical security to protect data and applications
- Offers a detailed backup and disaster recovery plan

With these things taken into account, it becomes very evident that maintaining direct control over everything comes at a high cost, and in most cases, those necessary elements are not met.

Alternative Delivery Models

Many customers remain concerned about control for good reasons. Consider national defense data, which must be carefully guarded with the absolute greatest security measures. You may think that national defense data isn't a good candidate for cloud computing, but it could be used effectively here too. It's actually possible to employ cloud computing technologies, such as virtualization and platforms on internal networks within a firewall. In doing so, customers can enjoy many of the benefits of cloud computing while minimizing the risks. Along those lines, NIST has suggested the term "public cloud" for a traditional Internet cloud, and suggests three alternative deployment models described below:

- **Private cloud (enterprise owned or managed)** - Private cloud (also called internal cloud or corporate cloud) is a term for an in-house cloud computing architecture that provides services to a limited number of people behind a corporate firewall. Private clouds are marketed to organizations that want more control over their data than they can get by using a third-party hosted service such as Amazon's Elastic Compute Cloud (EC2) or Simple Storage Service (S3).

- **Community cloud (shared infrastructure for specific community)** – Similar to a private cloud, except shared by several organizations with overlapping concerns. For example, NASA's Nebula offering may be considered as a federal community cloud.

- **Hybrid cloud (composition of two or more clouds)** – Refers to a cloud infrastructure that consists of two or more clouds (private, community, or public) that remain unique entities but are bound together by standardized or proprietary technology that enables data and application portability (e.g., cloud bursting for load-balancing between clouds).

Accessing the cloud

Making the move from on-premises applications and data storage to cloud-based applications and data storage is a big step, and one of the first things that comes to mind is *access*. "Can I get to my data and apps?" "Will there be latency and delay?" These are important questions. In the old days of centralized mainframe computing, and in the early days of networking, latency was common. Data entry people suffered productivity loss because they had to wait for processing on the back end before they could enter more data; applications were less responsive; and web surfing when the web was new could be a frustrating experience. Remember the first time you tried to access a graphical web site over a dial-up line? We think of those experiences and imagine cloud computing to be more of the same.

But the fact is, broadband access and gigabit-speed networking has changed all that, and the widespread access of broadband is the natural precursor of widespread cloud computing.

The details: How to buy it

We've painted a broad picture now of cloud computing, what it is, what it does, and how it helps us. But once you've made the decision to deploy cloud technology, then all of a sudden you're faced with the details. RFPs, needs analyses, sorting through the different vendors, watching their presentations and making a decision.

The process is the same as with any other type of technology. Determine what you need, put out an RFP, create a short list, and look at the offers. But one of the most important elements of purchasing cloud services is the service level agreement (SLA). An SLA has long been an important aspect of any sort of IT service, but in the era of the cloud, it becomes even more vital since so much more depends on the service.

The first thing to evaluate is whether the cloud service provider offers an SLA, and what the details of it may be. There are performance promises that are nothing more than marketing fluff: "Great service or your money back!" And then there are performance promises that have teeth. The SLA should include in specific language, at least the following:

- Expected performance levels should be laid out in specific terms.
- Uptime percentage must also be stated in specific numeric values.
- Response time should also be stated in specific terms.
- The provider should also provide for consequences if the terms are not met; for example, a penalty, free service for a period of time, etc.
- The SLA may also set out specific tasks and deliverables, such as reports or other functions.

Most cloud providers will offer a boilerplate SLA, and this may well be adequate—but if you are a large customer, tweaking the terms of the SLA is common. In some cases, the terms are negotiable.

Cloud providers, and other types of providers as well, have embraced the value of the SLA, not just because it delivers value to the customer, but for their own uses as well. From the perspective of the provider, it protects against escalating client expectations. For example, some services may deliver varying levels of guarantees, each one with a different rate. There may be for example, one price for a 98 percent guarantee, and another for a 99 percent guarantee.

XII. The Future of Cloud

Resistance to new technology concepts is inevitable, and cloud computing is no exception. But today, cloud computing has matured to the level where it is a viable technology, ready to embrace and bring benefit to your company.

The reasons why cloud computing's time is now include:

- Economic necessity
- Support from major mainstream software vendors
- Demand from small business for high-end features
- Demand from enterprise users for more cost-effective solutions
- Need for collaborative tools
- Cloud technology has already passed the proving ground stage

Economically, the market today is not only ready for cloud computing, it demands cloud computing. On a macro level, the world is facing a huge recession from which it will be slow to recover, and businesses of all sizes need an edge just to stay competitive. Increasing revenues is always a key strategy of any business, but the reality of the situation is that many companies are not able to do so in a struggling economy. This leaves only cost cutting as a way to stay flat or increase the bottom line.

When a business needs to cut expenses, it's not prudent to cut those areas that contribute to the company's overall mission. Staff reductions may provide a short-term shot in the arm, but in the long run, this may be detrimental. The better strategy in cost-cutting is to re-evaluate the company's technological underpinnings, and implement new technology that allows them to do more with less. Cloud computing is such a technology.

Furthermore, mainstream software vendors have all staked a claim in the cloud computing market. Enterprise software vendors, many with reputations for massively expensive implementations that take months or years to install successfully, have already rolled out cloud-based versions of their otherwise bulky systems. The results have been astounding. Enterprises have been using cloud-based versions of ERP software for example, to get up and running on individual modules immediately, instead of having to wait months for a custom rollout. Even if an on-premises solution is ultimately desired, the cloud-based system allows them to make an easier transition—and one of the hardest things about a major ERP installation is the transition. On the lower end, midsized businesses are taking advantage of these cloud-based enterprise systems to get functionality that they couldn't afford before they became available on the cloud. On the low end of the market, small businesses and SOHO companies also have the cloud at their disposal as well, with offerings from mainstream vendors like Microsoft, Google, and even Apple delivering a wide range of cloud-based applications and services that promote not only productivity, but increased collaboration as well.

The consumer market is especially important for the acceptance of cloud computing, as this is where the technology initially filters into the business mainstream. Consumers that have become accustomed to using Google

Apps, Microsoft Live, and Apple MobileMe will demand the same functionality in the workplace.

The collaborative potential is just as important as the functionality of the applications themselves. The fact that the cloud promotes collaboration fits in well with today's ways of doing business. The decentralization of the workplace, the growth of outsourcing, and the desire for telecommuting and work-at-home solutions all demand collaborative technologies to work, and this is now possible only through cloud computing technology.

And finally, we have to look at the adopter stage of any technology. Early adopters jump in when a technology is new and unproven, and serve the purpose of providing a testing ground for the rest of us. Today, we see that cloud computing has a rich collection of providers, both well-established and startup; and that users come from all segments and all business size classifications. Furthermore, cloud computing providers have expanded to encompass the entire range of cloud computing technology (infrastructure, platform, and application), with prominent vendors already offering robust deliverables in all three categories. Cloud computing has passed that early adopter stage and is now entering the mainstream.

To technologists, the future of cloud computing is easy to understand, because we have the advantage of history. To truly understand the future of cloud computing technology, we merely need to examine the historical evolution of earlier computing platforms. The cloud is evolving in many of the same ways, with its infrastructure, platforms and software.

	Computing Platforms	
	Desktop	**Cloud**
Year	1980s	2010
Infrastructure	PC (Intel/Seagate)	IaaS (Amazon)
OS	Unix/Windows	PaaS
Apps	Software Apps	SaaS
Interface	Platform API	Platform API
Functions	Subroutines	Web services
Modules	Custom Controls	J2EE Components
RAD Tools	VisiCalc	Cloud IDE

The cloud is evolving in the same ways as prior computing platforms

More important is the effect of the cloud on the people who use it. We may even say that cloud computing is reaching "critical mass." That is, it has come too far to put it back in the bottle. It's here, the technology is ready, and it is already making dramatic changes to the way people do business, the way we work, and even the way we think. It is creating a new class of entrepreneurs and ushering a second dotcom boom.

What are the implications of this technology achieving critical mass? For one, IT buyers will not need to defend why they are buying cloud computing services—the argument instead will focus on "why are you using antiquated technologies?" and "Why are you spending ten times too much on this project when you could be using cloud computing instead?"

Top ten predictions: The future of cloud computing

This new era of cloud computing is behind some of the biggest shifts in business since the Industrial Revolution. Today, the genie is out of the bottle, and change is imminent and inevitable. We're not alone in predicting a major role for cloud computing. Gartner placed cloud computing at the very top of its "Top Ten strategic technology areas for 2010" report, and virtually every research organization and think tank has declared it to be a technology that is destined to change the way we think about computing.

There is no doubt that as a disruptive technology, cloud computing's future is assured, but what will that future be? Following are ten predictions for how cloud computing will play into the future.

1. **Cloud infrastructure commoditizes, and prices fall.**

   Cloud computing already provides a pricing advantage to end users, who gain access to high-end applications at entry-level prices. But the infrastructure, upon which the rest of the cloud lives, will also decrease in price as more major players enter into the market to provide commodity infrastructures to hold the increasing number of cloud applications. Meanwhile, the competition is steepening. Together, this will make it even cheaper for applications providers to enter into the market.

2. **Open standards emerge as dominant in cloud platforms.**

   Cloud-based development becomes simpler, giving rise to greater competition from smaller players. It's "déjà vu all over again" as the proprietary shakeout gives way to open systems. These open systems not only simplify development and provide for more robust applications, they allow for a greater level of customization, and they also answer the vexing question of what happens to an application if a provider goes out of business.

3. **Homesourcing becomes mainstream.**

   Cloud computing will drag us kicking and screaming out of our cubicles and into our homes. There will be resistance on several fronts, but the move is inevitable due to the incredible efficiency gains and cost savings to companies. Because applications and data no longer need to reside on the computer in front of us, the physical office is quickly becoming redundant.

4. **Corporate processes become decentralized.**

   Larger companies take advantage of the decentralization made possible by cloud computing. This leads to a greater level of outsourcing, which in turns triggers the need for more smaller companies to fill the need for those outsourced services.

5. **A new wave of entrepreneurship emerges.**

   Cloud computing ushers in the next great dotcom boom, only this time things are different. Cloud computing has lowered the barriers to entry so that anyone can be a dotcom superstar. Entrepreneurs won't need to be programming wizards or venture backed. They only need an idea, ambition and a credit card.

6. **Smart phones evolve with cloud apps.**

   Smart phones like the iPhone and BlackBerry continue to gain functionality and power, and their reach extends further with easier access to wireless broadband. This makes smart phones more attractive as an actual working machine, and a tool for accessing productivity apps over the cloud for corporate use.

7. **The days of multi-million dollar enterprise software projects comes to an end.**

   Those years-long deployments, high failure rates and big price tags are already pushing their limits, and enterprise customers are demanding something better. Enterprise-level cloud computing apps will gradually replace those huge on-premises implementations with a more modular approach; and the existence of cloud platforms will encourage new entrants into the enterprise market. The days of multi-million IT projects will eventually fall by the wayside along with the fall of ground-up Web 2.0 engineering. Think about it – who, these days, would want to write an e-commerce website from the ground up when you can rent an e-commerce server? Yesterday's million dollar systems only cost a few dollars today. Likewise, cloud platforms will become the norm rather than the exception. The same thing is happening with other types of platforms, from social platforms to enterprise business systems.

8. **Cloud computing penetrates all areas of business management.**

   The earliest applications delivered more consumer-oriented applications and services, although cloud computing is by no means a consumer-only technology. Already in widespread use by SOHO and small businesses, it is expanding into larger enterprises. The result will be that cloud applications will evolve to accommodate more mission-critical needs, delivering full-fledged management systems to the largest government agencies and corporations in the world.

9. Big-name companies struggle for new identities.

Something fascinating happens when computing platforms change: the big IT boats get rocked. Hello IBM, do you remember that little company named Microsoft? Hello Microsoft, do you remember that little company named Google? Hello Facebook, do you remember that little company named??? The emergence of new cloud offerings from names like Rackspace will drive competition in the cloud infrastructure arena. Cloud platforms are enabling 10s of thousands of software newcomers. Cloud platforms will gain attention from infrastructure providers looking for new competitive advantages. In the end, several new brands will emerge, both from established players and newcomers to the market. The space will become more cluttered before eventually shaking out.

10. Social networking systems will evolve into collaborative management systems.

Today's managers need to get things done despite growing challenges. Their teams are more scattered and complex... more difficult to motivate, coordinate and hold accountable. An honest manager will tell you that real work is still being done with spreadsheets and emails. For these reasons and more, the future of collaboration will be more focused on the emerging needs of mangers who are coping with more complexity and demands. They need more than social networking. They need interactive management systems with real reports.

What's Next?

The future is unfolding quickly. It has been said that 1 year in computer technology is like 10 years in the automobile industry.

In the 1980s, PC computing showed us just how fast new computing technologies can reach the world. Cloud computing will move much faster, because it has several advantage, including today's Internet.

In a few years, we will go to our cloud desktop. It will probably look a lot like today's PC desktop. The underlying technologies will be different, but we'll leave those details to the techies. Soon, the hype will subside, but the cloud will be here to stay. We will use it without thinking about it.

We'll simply log on to do whatever we do.

About the Authors

Cary Landis owns and operates Virtual Global, Inc., where he currently serves as lead architect for the TeamHost™ enterprise cloud platform. In the past, Cary has engineered nationally-deployed software systems for federal agencies, including the US Department of Health and Human Services (HHS) / Food and Drug Administration (FDA), National Institute of Standards and Technology (NIST) and NASA. He also co-founded KeyLogic Systems. Cary currently resides in Morgantown, WV.

http://www.virtualglobal.com
http://www.teamhost.com

Dan Blacharski is a freelance writer, having published numerous books and articles for technology trade and popular press. He currently owns and operates Ugly Dog Media out of his virtual office in South Bend, Indiana with his wife, Charoenkwan. While in Silicon Valley, Dan created content for, and helped many dotcom startups fine-tune their messaging strategies, and had an opportunity to see first-hand what works, what doesn't, and what still gets supported even though it defies all common sense.

http://www.uglydogmedia.com

Index

Amazon, 12, 19, 34, 89

as-a-service, 11, 12, 13, 25, 31, 32, 34, 35, 49, 67

Benefits, 25

bloatware, 44

Cloud Infrastructure, 11, 19

Cloud Platforms, 11, 24, 25, 28

Cloud Software, 11, 31

collaboration, 8, 12, 38, 42, 44, 56, 61, 67, 68, 69, 76, 94, 100

Collaboration, 41, 58

Community cloud, 89

data center, 17, 21, 22, 46, 86, 88

elasticity, 13, 25

enterprise software, 17, 27, 29, 47, 48, 49, 50, 98

Facebook, 12, 29, 48

grid computing, 35, 52

Health-IT, 71

HIT, 73

HPC, 34, 35

Hybrid cloud, 90

IaaS, 11, 19

Infrastructure-as-a-Service, 11, 19

mainframes, 45

Middleware, 28, 69

NASA, 30, 75, 76, 83, 90, 102

Nebula, 75, 76, 90

NIST, 7, 12, 18, 19, 26, 84, 89, 102

offshoring, 56

on-demand, 13, 18

Open source, 77, 79

operating systems, 10, 11, 30, 37, 54, 83

PaaS, 11, 24

PC, 9, 10, 14, 21, 30, 40, 46, 54

Platform-as-a-Service, 11, 24

Private cloud, 89

risks, 24, 26, 28, 50, 80, 86, 89

SaaS, 7, 11, 26, 31, 32, 33, 42, 44, 49, 50, 54, 82

Scalability, 41

Security, 7, 80, 81, 82, 87

Simplicity, 41

SLA, 87, 88, 91, 92

SOAP, 33

Software as a Service, 7

SOHO, 6, 44, 49, 94, 99

supercomputing, 34
teleworking, 59
total cost of ownership, 29
Virtualization, 17, 22, 23, 42

Web 2.0, 42, 56, 61, 69, 98
web services, 25, 33
Windows, 9, 15, 31, 42, 83
XML, 33

Made in the USA
San Bernardino, CA
21 August 2015